A AK

Mutual Funds: The Masala in Your Financial Thali

A Bollywood-Style Guide to Indian Investing

Copyright © 2024 by A AK

All rights reserved. No part of this publication may be reproduced, stored or transmitted in any form or by any means, electronic, mechanical, photocopying, recording, scanning, or otherwise without written permission from the publisher. It is illegal to copy this book, post it to a website, or distribute it by any other means without permission.

First edition

This book was professionally typeset on Reedsy. Find out more at reedsy.com

Contents

Preface: Mutual Funds in India – A Bollywood-Style Financial...	ix
1 From Piggy Banks to Mutual Funds: Your Financial Journey...	1
Introduction to the concept of saving and investing	2
Saving: It's Not Just for Grandpas	2
Investing: Making Your Money Hustle	3
Compound Interest: The Magic Money Multiplier	3
Mutual Funds: Investing Made Easy	4
Why Should You Care?	5
Brief history of mutual funds in India	5
The OG Days: Enter Unit Trust of India (UTI)	6
The 1987 Plot Twist: Public Sector Joins the Party	6
The 1993 Big Bang: Private Players Enter, Stage Left	7
SEBI Enters: The Strict But Fair Teacher	7
The 2000s and Beyond: Mutual Funds Ka Jadoo Chha Gaya	8
The "Mutual Funds Sahi Hai" Era	8
Today: Bigger Than a Bollywood Box Office	9
2 Demystifying Mutual Funds: As Easy as Making Masala Chai	10
Basic explanation of mutual funds	11

What's a Mutual Fund Anyway?	11
How Does It Work? The Masala Chai Method	11
Mutual Fund Masala: Key Ingredients (Terms) You Should Know	12
Types of Mutual Funds: Flavors for Every Palate	13
Mutual Fund Masala 1: The Blockbuster Edition	14
Scene 1: The Unit-ed Nations	14
Scene 2: NAV-igating the Waters	14
Scene 3: The Great Indian Expense Ratio	15
Scene 4: AUMazing Race	15
Scene 5: Dividend Dhamaka	16
Scene 6: The Exit Load-lock	16
Scene 7: SIP: Chai Pe Charcha	16
Climax: The Mutual Fund Mahabharata	17
Mutual Fund Masala 2: The Flavor Frenzy	17
Scene 1: The Equity Express	18
Scene 2: The Debt Dhaba	18
Scene 3: The Hybrid Haveli	19
Scene 4: The Index Imitation Game	20
Scene 5: The Sectoral Mela	20
Climax: The Fund of Funds Finale	21
Mutual Fund Masala 3: Return of the Investment	22
Scene 1: The Return Rollercoaster	22
Scene 2: The Risk Rapids	23
Scene 3: The Benchmark Bhangra	24
Scene 4: The Expense Ratio Escape Room	24
Scene 5: The Tracking Error Trail	25
Climax: The Performance Evaluation Palace	25
Mutual Fund Masala 4: The Quest for the Perfect Portfolio	26
Scene 1: The Asset Allocation Arena	26

Scene 2: The Diversification Bazaar	27
Scene 3: The Rebalancing Seesaw	28
Scene 4: The Goal-Based Treasure Hunt	28
Scene 5: The SIP Waterfall	29
Climax: The Portfolio Management Palace	30
Mutual Fund Masala: The Great Indian Savings Race	30
Scene 1: The Starting Line	31
Scene 2: The Short Sprint (1-3 years)	31
Scene 3: The Middle Distance (3-7 years)	32
Scene 4: The Long Haul (7+ years)	32
Scene 5: The Inflation Hurdles	33
Scene 6: The Tax Trap	33
Climax: The Finish Line	34
3 Stocks vs. Mutual Funds: The Daal and Roti of Indian...	36
Scene 1: The Kitchen Introduction	37
Scene 2: The Recipe (How They Work)	37
Scene 3: The Taste Test (Returns)	38
Scene 4: The Kitchen Chaos (Risk Management)	38
Scene 5: The Budget (Minimum Investment)	39
Scene 6: The Cooking Time (Time and Effort)	39
Scene 7: The Masala Mix (Diversification)	40
Climax: The Grand Buffet	40
4 The Great Indian Mutual Fund Bazaar: Types for Every Taste	42
Scene 1: Entering the Bazaar	43
Scene 2: Equity Street	43
Scene 3: Debt Boulevard	44
Scene 4: Hybrid Haveli	45
Scene 5: The Index Imitation Alley	46

Scene 6: Sectoral Specialties Square	46
Climax: The Fund of Funds Food Court	47
5 Tech Tadka: The Spice of Modern Mutual Fund Investing	49
Scene 1: Entering the Tech Tadka Expo	50
Scene 2: The Mobile App Mela	50
Scene 3: The Robo-Advisor Raj	51
Scene 4: The Digital KYC Dhaba	52
Scene 5: The SIP Automation Station	53
Scene 6: The Analytics Adda	53
Climax: The Virtual Reality Investing Theater	54
6 Choosing Your Perfect Mutual Fund: Like Finding Your...	56
Scene 1: Entering the Fund Feast	57
Scene 2: The Risk Appetite Meter	57
Scene 3: The Financial Goals Thali	58
Scene 4: The Return Expectation Juice Bar	59
Scene 5: The Diversification Chaat Corner	59
Scene 6: The Fund Manager's Kitchen	60
Scene 7: The Expense Ratio Weighing Scale	60
Climax: Crafting Your Perfect Financial Menu	61
7 The Art of Investing: Timing Your Entry Like a Mumbai Local	63
Scene 1: Entering Churchgate Station	64
Scene 2: The Lump Sum Express	64
Scene 3: The SIP Local Train	65
Scene 4: The Rupee-Cost Averaging Junction	66
Scene 5: The Value Averaging Fast Local	66
Scene 6: The Market Timing Express	67
Scene 7: The Long-Term Investor's Duronto	67
Climax: Choosing Your Investment Route	68

8 Navigating the Markets: Your GPS Through Bull and Bear...	70
Scene 1: Entering the Financial Forest	71
Scene 2: The Bull Run Boulevard	71
Scene 3: The Bear Cave Descent	72
Scene 4: The Value Valley	73
Scene 5: The Cyclical Roundabout	73
Scene 6: The Volatility Rapids	74
Scene 7: The Economic Indicators Observatory	74
Climax: The All-Weather Portfolio Plains	75
9 Tax Savings: The Sweet Chutney of Mutual Fund Investing	77
Scene 1: The Financial Cuisine Kitchen	78
Scene 2: Cooking the ELSS Eclair	78
Scene 3: The Long-Term Capital Gains Lassi	79
Scene 4: The Debt Fund Dharana	80
Scene 5: The Dividend Dehaat	80
Scene 6: The Tax Harvesting Tadka	81
Climax: The Tax-Efficient Investment Thali	82
10 Common Pitfalls: Avoiding the Potholes on Your Investment...	83
Scene 1: The Investment Highway Departure	84
Scene 2: The Herd Mentality Hairpin Bend	84
Scene 3: The Short-Term Thinking Shortcut	85
Scene 4: The Diversification Desert	86
Scene 5: The Expense Ratio Expressway	86
Scene 6: The Panic Selling Pothole	87
Scene 7: The Research Roundabout	88
Climax: The Balanced Portfolio Bridge	88
11 Your Mutual Fund Toolkit: Essentials for Every Indian...	90

Scene 1: The Secret Briefing	91
Scene 2: The Research Radar	91
Scene 3: The Financial Ratio Analyzer	92
Scene 4: The AMC Archives	93
Scene 5: The Market News Multiverse	93
Scene 6: The Trading Terminal	94
Scene 7: The Regulatory Roundtable	95
Climax: The Mission Briefcase	96
12 Building Your Financial Thali: Balancing Mutual Funds in...	97
Scene 1: The Financial Kitchen	98
Scene 2: The Equity Entree	98
Scene 3: The Debt Daal	99
Scene 4: The Hybrid Halwa	100
Scene 5: The International Chutney	101
Scene 6: The Liquid Fund Raita	101
Scene 7: The Gold Fund Dessert	102
Climax: Assembling Your Financial Thali	102
13 The Road Ahead: Future of Mutual Funds in India	104
Scene 1: The Time Machine Launch	105
Scene 2: The Digital Revolution Plaza	105
Scene 3: The Sustainable Investing Skyway	106
Scene 4: The Crypto-Commodities Exchange	107
Scene 5: The Global Investment Gateway	107
Scene 6: The Micro-Investing Mela	108
Scene 7: The Regulatory Roundtable	108
Climax: The Future Finance Festival	109

Preface: Mutual Funds in India - A Bollywood-Style Financial Adventure

Dear Reader,

Namaste and welcome to "Mutual Funds: The Masala in Your Financial Thali"! If you've picked up this book expecting a dry, number-crunching treatise on mutual funds, prepare to be pleasantly surprised. What you hold in your hands (or perhaps are viewing on your screen) is nothing short of a Bollywood blockbuster in book form – minus the choreographed dance numbers, but with all the drama, excitement, and, dare I say, masala of a box office hit!

Why, you ask, would anyone want to turn mutual fund education into a Bollywood-style adventure? Well, why not? For far too long, the world of finance has been shrouded in jargon, intimidating graphs, and sleep-inducing presentations. It's time we changed that narrative, especially here in India, where our love for a good story is as deep as our desire for financial security.

In this book, we're going to take you on a whirlwind tour of the mutual fund landscape, but with a twist. Imagine learning about equity funds while navigating the bustling streets of Mumbai, or understanding risk management through a thrilling chase sequence. Picture yourself grasping the concept of diversification by crafting the perfect thali, or exploring fund selection as if you're choosing the cast for a blockbuster movie.

Our protagonist, **Mutual Kumar** (yes, we went there with the name), will be your guide through this financial adventure. Together, you'll face the villains of bad investment decisions, dance through the rain of market volatility, and ultimately emerge as the hero of your own financial story.

But don't let the entertainment factor fool you. Beneath the fun and games lies a wealth of solid, practical knowledge about mutual funds in the Indian context. We've taken great care to ensure that while you're laughing at our Bollywood-inspired scenarios, you're also absorbing crucial information that can help you make informed investment decisions.

From understanding the basics of how mutual funds work to navigating the complex world of fund selection, from tax-saving strategies to building a diversified portfolio, we cover it all. And we do it in a way that's not just palatable, but downright delicious – like a perfectly spiced biryani for your brain!

So, whether you're a mutual fund newbie looking to dip your toes in the investment pool, or a seasoned investor seeking a fresh perspective, this book has something for you. By the time you turn the last page, you'll not only have a solid grasp of mutual funds but also a few chuckles under your belt.

Remember, in the grand Bollywood movie of life, you're the star, and your financial well-being is the happily-ever-after we're aiming for. So grab your popcorn (or maybe some samosas), settle in, and get ready for "Mutual Funds: The Masala in Your Financial Thali" – where finance meets fun, and learning meets laughter!

Lights, camera, invest!
   A AK (Financial Edutainer and Author)

1

From Piggy Banks to Mutual Funds: Your Financial Journey Begins

From Piggy Banks to Prosperity: A Journey of Growth

Introduction to the concept of saving and investing

Hey there! Ready to talk about money without dozing off? Cool, let's dive in!

Saving: It's Not Just for Grandpas

Remember when you were a kid and got some cash from your aunt at Diwali? You probably had two choices: buy a bunch of chocolates or stash it in your piggy bank. That, my friend, was your first money decision!

Saving is just setting aside some cash for later. It's like packing an umbrella when the weather app says it might rain. You're just getting ready for what's coming.

Take my buddy Priya. She's in college and saves 500 bucks from her pocket money every month. By the time she's done with school, she's got enough saved up for a new phone. Pretty sweet, right?

But here's the thing – saving is just the start.

Investing: Making Your Money Hustle

Okay, so you've been saving. Good job! But let's kick it up a notch.

Investing is like planting a mango seed instead of just eating the mango. Sure, you could enjoy it now, but plant that seed and you'll have a whole tree of mangoes later!

Remember that uncle in your society who retired but still goes on nice holidays? Chances are he didn't just save – he invested. While everyone else was blowing cash on the latest stuff, he was putting money into things that grew over time, like mutual funds.

Compound Interest: The Magic Money Multiplier

Now, let's talk about something cool called compound interest. It's like a money-making snowball.

Here's how it works: You start with some cash, and it earns interest. Next year, you earn interest on your original cash PLUS the interest from last year. It keeps growing and growing!

Check this out:
  - Amit and Suman are twins. On their 25th birthday, they each get ₹10,000.
  - Amit puts his in a regular savings account earning 4% per

year.
 - Suman invests hers in a mutual fund that has historically given about 12% returns per year.

Fast forward 30 years:
 - Amit's ₹10,000 grew to about ₹32,400.
 - Suman's? It exploded to ₹300,000!

That's compound interest for you – it's like your money making babies!

Mutual Funds: Investing Made Easy

Now you might be thinking, "Sounds great, but I don't know squat about stocks and all that jazz." No worries! That's where mutual funds come in.

Think of mutual funds like carpooling, but for money. You chip in your cash with a bunch of other people. Then, a pro driver (aka a fund manager) takes that pooled money and invests it in a mix of stocks, bonds, and other stuff.

It's like ordering a thali instead of cooking each dish yourself. You get a bit of everything without all the hassle.

Why Should You Care?

Whether you're dreaming of buying a car, planning a wedding, or thinking about your kid's school fees, knowing how to grow your money is super important.

In the next chapters, we'll get into the nitty-gritty of mutual funds – how they tick, the different flavors available, and how you can use them to reach your money goals. Don't worry, we'll keep it fun and relatable!

Remember, building wealth is like prepping for a cricket match. You don't need to hit a six on every ball. You just need to keep scoring consistently.

So, ready to level up from your piggy bank? Let's roll!

Brief history of mutual funds in India

Alright, finance fans! Let's take a quick trip down memory lane and check out how mutual funds in India went from zero to hero. It's like a masala movie, but with more numbers and less dancing (sorry, not sorry!).

The OG Days: Enter Unit Trust of India (UTI)

Picture this: It's 1963. The Beatles are rocking the world, and India decides it's time to rock the financial world too. Enter Unit Trust of India (UTI), the OG of mutual funds in India.

UTI was like that cool kid in school who did something no one else was doing. It launched Unit Scheme 1964, India's first mutual fund scheme. People were like, "Wait, what? We can invest together? Cool!"

For a long time, UTI was the lone ranger in the mutual fund rodeo. It was like having only one flavor of ice cream – better than no ice cream, but come on, we need options!

The 1987 Plot Twist: Public Sector Joins the Party

Fast forward to 1987. India's ready to spice things up. Public sector banks and insurance companies crash the mutual fund party. It's like when your cousins show up at a family function – suddenly, things get interesting!

SBI Mutual Fund and Canbank Mutual Fund strutted onto the scene. LIC, GIC, and PNB soon followed. The mutual fund world was growing faster than your dad's WhatsApp group!

The 1993 Big Bang: Private Players Enter, Stage Left

1993 rolls around, and boom! Private sector and foreign companies get the green light to start mutual funds. It's like India opened the gates and said, "Come on in, the water's fine!"

Suddenly, we've got more mutual fund options than types of dosas at a South Indian restaurant. Kothari Pioneer (now merged with Franklin Templeton) becomes the first private player to say "Hello, India!"

SEBI Enters: The Strict But Fair Teacher

In 1996, the Securities and Exchange Board of India (SEBI) struts in like a strict school principal. They're all, "Okay, kids, time for some rules."

SEBI starts regulating mutual funds, making sure everyone plays nice. It's like having a referee in a gully cricket match – keeps things fair and stops that one guy from always claiming he's "not out."

The 2000s and Beyond: Mutual Funds Ka Jadoo Chha Gaya

As we hit the 2000s, mutual funds in India are hotter than a plate of sizzling brownies. New types of funds pop up faster than startups in Bangalore. We've got equity funds, debt funds, hybrid funds – more varieties than you can shake a stick at!

Technology joins the party, making it easier to invest. Suddenly, buying mutual funds is as easy as ordering a pizza on Swiggy.

The "Mutual Funds Sahi Hai" Era

In 2017, the Association of Mutual Funds in India (AMFI) launches the now-famous "Mutual Funds Sahi Hai" campaign. It's like the "Got Milk?" of the finance world – simple, catchy, and everywhere!

This campaign does for mutual funds what Maggi did for 2-minute noodles – makes them a household name. Suddenly, everyone from your techie cousin to your sabziwala is talking about mutual funds.

Today: Bigger Than a Bollywood Box Office

Today, the Indian mutual fund industry is bigger than Shah Rukh Khan's fan club (okay, maybe not that big, but you get the idea). With over ₹40 lakh crore in assets under management as of 2023, it's safe to say mutual funds have become a blockbuster hit!

From one lonely player in 1963 to a star-studded industry today, mutual funds in India have come a long way. It's like watching a skinny kid grow up to be a Bollywood heartthrob – the transformation is amazing!

So there you have it, folks – the story of mutual funds in India. From humble beginnings to a nationwide sensation, it's been quite a ride. And guess what? This blockbuster is still running, and you're invited to be part of the sequel!

2

Demystifying Mutual Funds: As Easy as Making Masala Chai

Chai & Charts: Brewing the Basics of Mutual Funds

Basic explanation of mutual funds

Alright, chai lovers! Let's brew up some mutual fund knowledge that's as comforting as your favorite cuppa. Don't worry, we won't use any fancy financial jargon without explaining it first. Promise!

What's a Mutual Fund Anyway?

Imagine you and your gang decide to throw a massive Diwali party. Instead of one person bearing all the cost (and stress!), everyone chips in some cash. You pool the money and assign the most party-savvy friend to handle everything. That's basically a mutual fund!

In finance lingo: A mutual fund is a pool of money collected from many investors to invest in stocks, bonds, or other assets. A professional money manager (our party-savvy friend) takes care of investing this pool of money.

How Does It Work? The Masala Chai Method

Think of a mutual fund like making masala chai for a big group:

1. **Ingredients (Money)**: Just like you need tea leaves, milk, water, and spices, a mutual fund needs money from different investors.
2. **The Chef (Fund Manager)**: The fund manager is like the chai expert in your family. They know just how to mix everything to get the best flavor (returns).
3. **The Recipe (Investment Strategy)**: This is how the fund manager decides to invest the money. Some might go

heavy on the ginger (stocks), others might prefer more cardamom (bonds).
4. **The Final Product (Portfolio)**: This is what you end up with – a perfect blend of investments that (hopefully) tastes great and warms your wallet!

Mutual Fund Masala: Key Ingredients (Terms) You Should Know

Now, let's spice things up with some must-know mutual fund terms. Don't worry, we'll keep it simpler than your mom's secret biryani recipe!

1. **Units**: Think of these as slices of a cake. When you invest in a mutual fund, you're buying these slices. The more money you invest, the more slices (units) you get.
2. **Net Asset Value (NAV)**: This is like the price tag on each slice of cake. It's calculated daily and tells you the value of each unit of the mutual fund.
3. **Expense Ratio**: Remember that chai-wallah who makes amazing cutting chai? He charges for his skill, right? Same here. This is the annual fee the fund charges for managing your money. It's like the chai-wallah's tip, but it comes out of your returns.
4. **Assets Under Management (AUM)**: This is the total size of the mutual fund cake. It's all the money that all investors have put into the fund.
5. **Dividend**: It's like when your favorite aunty sends you some extra cash on your birthday. Some mutual funds might give you a share of their profits regularly.
6. **Exit Load**: This is the party pooper of mutual funds. If

you leave the party (withdraw your money) too early, you might have to pay a small fee. It's like cancellation charges, but for investments.
7. **Systematic Investment Plan (SIP)**: This is like a chai subscription. Instead of buying a whole lot at once, you invest a fixed amount regularly. It's perfect for those who can't afford a big lump sum or want to invest steadily.

Types of Mutual Funds: Flavors for Every Palate

Just like there are different types of chai (masala, ginger, cardamom), there are different types of mutual funds. Here's a quick taste:

1. **Equity Funds**: These are the masala chai of mutual funds – bold and potentially rewarding. They invest mainly in stocks.
2. **Debt Funds**: Think of these as green tea – generally calmer and steadier. They invest in bonds and other fixed-income securities.
3. **Hybrid Funds**: These are like mixed chai – a blend of stocks and bonds. Best of both worlds!
4. **Index Funds**: These try to copy a market index, like the Sensex. It's like following your grandma's exact chai recipe without adding your own twist.
5. **Sector Funds**: These focus on specific industries, like tech or healthcare. It's like specializing in only Irani chai or cutting chai.

Remember, just like how some people prefer their chai super sweet while others like it kadak, different mutual funds suit different people. It all depends on your taste (financial goals) and how much heat (risk) you can handle!

Ready to take a sip of the mutual fund world? Let's keep brewing this knowledge kadak-style in the next chapters!

Mutual Fund Masala 1: The Blockbuster Edition

Ladies and gentlemen, boys and girls! Get ready for the financial thriller of the year: "Mutual Fund Masala: Decoding the Da Pinchi Code"! Starring our hero, Mutual Kumar, as he unravels the mysteries of the mutual fund world!

Scene 1: The Unit-ed Nations

Mutual Kumar walks into a bustling market. A chaiwala shouts, "Units! Get your mutual fund units here!"

Kumar: "What are these units, chaiwala ji?"

Chaiwala: "Oh simple! Imagine you're buying pieces of a giant jalebi. The more money you give, the more pieces you get. We call these sweet pieces 'units'. Invest ₹1000 when each piece costs ₹20, you get 50 pieces. Yummy math, no?"

Lesson: Units are your share of the mutual fund. The number you get depends on how much you invest and the cost per unit.

Scene 2: NAV-igating the Waters

Kumar now boards a boat named "NAV Express". The captain announces, "Today's NAV is ₹24.50!"

Kumar: "Captain, what's this NAV?"

Captain: "NAV is 'Net Asset Value', my boy! It's like checking how much water is in our boat every day. We add up all the goodies in our boat, subtract any holes (debts), and divide by the number of passengers. That gives us the ticket price – I mean, the NAV – for one seat on this financial cruise!"

Lesson: NAV is calculated daily and represents the per-unit value of the mutual fund.

Scene 3: The Great Indian Expense Ratio

Kumar enters a store named "Expense Ratio Emporium". The shopkeeper greets him.

Shopkeeper: "Welcome to the only shop where we tell you exactly how much we're overcharging!"

Kumar: "Eh?"

Shopkeeper: "See, we manage your money, right? For that, we charge a small fee. If our expense ratio is 1% and you invested ₹10,000, we take ₹100. Fair and transparent, like a glass of clean ganga jal!"

Lesson: Expense Ratio is the annual fee charged by the fund, expressed as a percentage of your investment.

Scene 4: AUMazing Race

Kumar joins a race where runners carry bags of money. The announcer yells, "On your mark, get set, AUM!"

Kumar: "AUM? Like the meditation chant?"

Runner: "No, silly! AUM means 'Assets Under Management'. See all this money we're carrying? The total value is our AUM. The bigger our money bag, the higher our AUM!"

Lesson: AUM represents the total market value of all the investments managed by a mutual fund.

Scene 5: Dividend Dhamaka

Kumar attends a grand Dividend Mela. People are celebrating as money rains from the sky.

Kumar: "Wow! Free money!"

Wise Old Man: "Not so fast, young man. That's dividend – a share of profits some funds distribute. But remember, it's like breaking a piece of your gold biscuit and giving it back to you. Your total gold remains the same!"

Lesson: Dividends are distributions of fund profits, but they come from your own investment.

Scene 6: The Exit Load-lock

Kumar tries to leave the Mutual Fund Mela but faces a tollbooth.

Tollbooth Operator: "Oi! Leaving so soon? That'll be 1% exit load, please!"

Kumar: "Exit load? But I just entered!"

Operator: "That's the rule, boss. Leave the party too early, you pay a small fee. Stay longer, party for free!"

Lesson: Exit Load is a fee charged if you withdraw your investment before a specified period.

Scene 7: SIP: Chai Pe Charcha

Kumar sits with his friends at a tapri, sipping cutting chai.

Friend: "Aye Kumar, want to join our SIP?"

Kumar: "Systematic Investment Plan, right? Like a chai subscription?"

Friend: "Exactly! Instead of splurging ₹5000 on premium Darjeeling tea once, we invest ₹500 every month in this awesome chai stall. Regular investment, better returns, no indigestion!"

Lesson: SIP allows you to invest a fixed amount regularly instead of a large sum at once.

Climax: The Mutual Fund Mahabharata

In the epic finale, Kumar faces the final boss: Understanding Mutual Funds Completely!

Kumar: "I've learned so much! Units, NAV, Expense Ratio, AUM, Dividends, Exit Loads, SIPs... But how do I choose the right fund?"

Mysterious Voice: "Ah, for that you need to understand fund types, asset allocation, risk assessment, and much more! But that, dear Kumar, is a story for another movie..."

To be continued...

And there you have it, folks! Our hero Mutual Kumar has unraveled the basics of mutual funds. Remember, just like in the movies, every mutual fund has its own story, full of twists and turns. Your job is to find the one with the happiest ending for your money!

Now, go forth and invest wisely! And don't forget the popcorn!

Mutual Fund Masala 2: The Flavor Frenzy

Welcome back to the blockbuster world of mutual funds! In this thrilling sequel, our hero Mutual Kumar explores the wild and wacky world of mutual fund types. Grab your popcorn and get ready for "Types of Mutual Funds: Flavors for Every Palate"!

Scene 1: The Equity Express

Mutual Kumar enters a bustling train station. He spots a luxurious train with "Equity Express" written on it.

Station Master: "All aboard the Equity Express! High risk, high reward!"

Kumar: "Sounds exciting! But what's this train about?"

Station Master: "This train invests mainly in company stocks. It's like booking a ticket on a rocket ship. You might reach the moon, or you might need a parachute. But over long journeys, it often beats other trains!"

Types to know:

1. Large-cap: The first-class compartment. Stable, but tickets are expensive!
2. Mid-cap: The middle berth. More exciting ride, but might make you dizzy.
3. Small-cap: The engine cab. Super thrilling, but not for the faint-hearted!

Lesson: Equity funds invest in stocks. They're generally for long-term investors who can stomach some risk.

Scene 2: The Debt Dhaba

Kumar feels hungry and stops at a roadside dhaba named "Debt Dhaba: Fixed Income Foods".

Dhaba Owner: "Welcome to Debt Dhaba! We serve safe, steady meals. No indigestion guaranteed!"

Kumar: "Sounds bland. What's on the menu?"

Dhaba Owner: "We've got government bond biryani, corporate FD curry, and money market manchurian. Less spicy than equity, but at least you won't get dehshat in your pet (terror in your stomach)!"

Types to know:

1. Government Securities Funds: As safe as mom's home-cooked food.
2. Corporate Bond Funds: Like eating at a nice restaurant. Tastier returns, but check the restaurant's reputation!
3. Liquid Funds: Our fast food option. Quick and easy, perfect for short-term hunger.

Lesson: Debt funds invest in fixed-income securities. They're generally safer but offer lower returns than equity funds.

Scene 3: The Hybrid Haveli

Kumar arrives at a grand haveli with a sign "Hybrid Harmony: Best of Both Worlds".

Guide: "Welcome to Hybrid Haveli! We've got a little bit of everything here."

Kumar: "So, it's not fully equity or debt?"

Guide: "Exactly! It's like having dal and chawal. Some rooms are filled with equity excitement, others with debt calmness. Perfect for guests who want a balanced stay!"

Types to know:

1. Balanced Funds: Equal parts equity and debt. Like a perfect mix of sweet and salty in your trail mix.
2. Monthly Income Plans: More debt than equity. It's for uncles who want regular pocket money from their invest-

ments.

Lesson: Hybrid funds mix equity and debt in different proportions, offering a balance between risk and stability.

Scene 4: The Index Imitation Game

Kumar stumbles upon a street performance. Performers are mimicking passersby perfectly.

Kumar: "What's going on here?"

Performer: "We're the Index Imitators! We don't try to outsmart the market, we just copy it. See that guy in the blue shirt? He represents the Sensex. We'll mirror his every move!"

Types to know:

1. Index Funds: Copy a specific market index. It's like following a choreographed Bollywood dance sequence step by step.
2. Exchange Traded Funds (ETFs): Similar to index funds, but traded like stocks. It's like a dance video you can buy or sell anytime!

Lesson: Index funds and ETFs aim to replicate the performance of a specific market index, not beat it.

Scene 5: The Sectoral Mela

Kumar visits a mela where each stall represents a different industry.

Mela Organizer: "Welcome to the Sectoral Mela! Each stall here is a different sector of the economy."

Kumar: "So I can invest in specific sectors?"

Organizer: "Absolutely! Fancy tech? Visit the IT stall. Think healthcare is the future? We've got a pharma stall. But remember, putting all your money in one stall is like eating only jalebi for dinner. Tasty, but not balanced!"

Lesson: Sector funds focus on specific industries. They can offer high returns but also carry higher risk due to lack of diversification.

Climax: The Fund of Funds Finale

In the grand finale, Kumar discovers a massive theme park: "Fund of Funds Fantasia".

Park Manager: "This is it, Kumar! The ultimate mutual fund adventure. Each ride here is actually a collection of other mutual fund rides!"

Kumar: "So, I can experience multiple funds through one ticket?"

Manager: "Exactly! It's like a thali that lets you taste a bit of everything. Perfect for those who want diversification on steroids!"

Lesson: Fund of Funds invest in other mutual funds, offering a way to diversify across multiple funds with a single investment.

And cut! That's a wrap on our mutual fund type extravaganza. Remember, dear audience, just like choosing between action, comedy, or romance in movies, picking mutual funds depends on your personal taste, goals, and how much financial drama you can handle!

Mutual Fund Masala 3: Return of the Investment

Lights, camera, action! Welcome back to our blockbuster mutual fund series. In this thrilling installment, our hero Mutual Kumar learns about the most exciting part of mutual funds - the returns! But wait, there's a twist. He must also face the villain: Risk! Let the adventure begin!

Scene 1: The Return Rollercoaster

Kumar enters an amusement park called "Returnland". He approaches a massive rollercoaster named "The Return Rider".

Ride Operator: "Welcome to The Return Rider! Want to experience the ups and downs of mutual fund returns?"

Kumar: "Sounds thrilling! But how does it work?"

Operator: "Hop on and find out! Oh, and here's your 'Returns Report' - you'll need it later!"

Kumar rides the rollercoaster, experiencing exhilarating highs and stomach-churning lows.

Operator: "So, how was it?"

Kumar (dizzy): "Wow! Some parts were amazing, others... not so much."

Operator: "Exactly! That's mutual fund returns for you. Now, let's check your Returns Report."

Returns Report:

1. Absolute Return: You started at 100 feet and ended at 150 feet. That's a 50% absolute return!
2. Annualized Return: But the ride lasted 5 years. So your annualized return is about 8.45% per year.
3. CAGR (Compound Annual Growth Rate): This smooths out

the ups and downs, showing your consistent growth rate - also about 8.45% per year in this case.

Lesson: Returns can be measured in different ways. Absolute returns show total growth, while annualized returns and CAGR give a yearly perspective, useful for comparing investments over different time periods.

Scene 2: The Risk Rapids

Next, Kumar approaches a wild river rafting ride called "The Risk Rapids".

Guide: "Ready to face the Risk Rapids? It's right next to The Return Rider for a reason!"

Kumar: "Do I have a choice?"

Guide: "In investing? Not really! Higher returns often mean a bumpier ride. But don't worry, I'll teach you some safety moves."

They navigate through the rapids, with Kumar learning to handle the rough waters.

Guide: "Great job! Now, let's measure how wild your ride was with these risk meters."

Risk Meters:

1. Standard Deviation: Measures how much your returns fluctuated. High number = wild ride!
2. Beta: Compares your ride to the general river flow (market). Beta > 1 means your ride was wilder than average.
3. Sharpe Ratio: Checks if the thrills (returns) were worth the spills (risks). Higher is better!

Lesson: Understanding risk is crucial. It helps you decide if the potential returns are worth the roller coaster ride your stomach (and wallet) might endure.

Scene 3: The Benchmark Bhangra

Kumar enters a dance competition called "Benchmark Bhangra".

Host: "Welcome to Benchmark Bhangra! Here, we don't just dance - we compete against the market's moves!"

Kumar: "So, I'm not just performing, but trying to outdance someone?"

Host: "Exactly! Your mutual fund isn't just aiming for good returns, it's trying to beat a benchmark like the Sensex or Nifty. Let's dance!"

Kumar and other contestants dance, trying to outperform a professional dancer representing the benchmark.

Host: "Great moves, Kumar! You outdanced the benchmark by 2%! That's called Alpha - the extra performance over the benchmark. If you had underperformed, it would be negative Alpha. No pressure!"

Lesson: Benchmarks help you understand if your fund is performing well compared to the overall market or its peers.

Scene 4: The Expense Ratio Escape Room

Kumar finds himself in a tricky escape room.

Game Master: "Welcome to the Expense Ratio Escape Room! Your returns are locked in this room. To get out with maximum returns, you need to minimize your expenses. The clock is ticking!"

Kumar solves puzzles representing various fund expenses, trying to keep them as low as possible.

Game Master: "Congratulations! You escaped with an expense ratio of 1.5%. That means if your fund earned 10%, your actual return is 8.5%. Always check the expense ratio - it's silently nibbling at your returns!"

Lesson: The expense ratio directly affects your returns. Lower expenses mean more returns in your pocket.

Scene 5: The Tracking Error Trail

Kumar embarks on a hiking trail called "Tracking Error Trek".

Trail Guide: "This trail represents an index fund's journey. Your goal is to follow the marked path as closely as possible."

Kumar tries his best but occasionally deviates from the path.

Trail Guide: "Great effort! Your deviations from the path represent tracking error. For index funds and ETFs, lower tracking error is better - it means they're sticking closely to their benchmark."

Lesson: For index funds, tracking error shows how closely the fund follows its benchmark. Lower is generally better.

Climax: The Performance Evaluation Palace

Finally, Kumar reaches a grand palace where all his experiences come together.

Palace Keeper: "Welcome to the Performance Evaluation Palace! Here's where you use everything you've learned to choose winning funds."

Kumar uses his knowledge of returns, risks, benchmarks, expenses, and tracking error to navigate through the palace, evaluating different funds.

Palace Keeper: "Remember, Kumar, past performance doesn't guarantee future results. But understanding these concepts helps you make informed decisions!"

Final Lesson: Evaluating mutual funds involves looking at returns, understanding risks, comparing to benchmarks, considering expenses, and more. It's a holistic process!

And cut! That's a wrap on "Mutual Fund Masala 3: Return of the Investment". Remember, dear viewers, in the world of mutual funds, being a smart investor is the real happily ever after!

Mutual Fund Masala 4: The Quest for the Perfect Portfolio

Lights, camera, action! Welcome to the epic finale of our mutual fund blockbuster series. In this thrilling conclusion, our hero Mutual Kumar embarks on a quest to build the perfect mutual fund portfolio. Get ready for action, drama, and financial wisdom!

Scene 1: The Asset Allocation Arena

Kumar enters a massive arena with three gates: "Equity Empire", "Debt Domain", and "Cash Kingdom".

Arena Master: "Welcome to the Asset Allocation Arena! Your quest begins here. Choose your path wisely!"

Kumar: "But how do I decide which gate to enter?"

Arena Master: "Ah, that depends on your goals, time horizon, and risk tolerance. Let's find out!"

The Arena Master hands Kumar a magical mirror.

Arena Master: "Look into the mirror and answer truthfully: What are your financial goals? When do you need the money? How do you feel about risk?"

As Kumar answers, the mirror glows and shows a unique path through all three gates.

Arena Master: "Your path is revealed! You'll spend 70% of your time in Equity Empire, 25% in Debt Domain, and 5% in Cash Kingdom. This is your ideal asset allocation!"

Lesson: Asset allocation is the foundation of your portfolio. It's based on your personal financial situation and goals, not a one-size-fits-all approach.

Scene 2: The Diversification Bazaar

Kumar enters a bustling bazaar filled with various mutual fund stalls.

Bazaar Guide: "Welcome to the Diversification Bazaar! Here, we follow the age-old wisdom: Don't put all your eggs in one basket!"

Kumar: "So, I should buy from every stall?"

Bazaar Guide: "Not necessarily. The trick is to choose a mix that balances your risks and returns. Let's shop!"

They visit stalls representing different types of mutual funds:

1. Large-cap Lassi: Steady and reliable
2. Mid-cap Masala Dosa: Spicier but with growth potential
3. Small-cap Sev Puri: Exciting but unpredictable
4. International Investing Ice Cream: A taste of global flavors
5. Debt Dahi Vada: Cool and comforting
6. Balanced Bhel Puri: A mix of everything

Bazaar Guide: "Remember, diversification isn't just about quantity, it's about choosing funds that complement each other!"

Lesson: Diversification helps manage risk by spreading your investments across different types of assets and funds.

Scene 3: The Rebalancing Seesaw

Kumar approaches a giant seesaw in a park.

Park Keeper: "Welcome to the Rebalancing Seesaw! Over time, your portfolio might tilt out of balance. Your job is to keep it level."

Kumar hops on the seesaw, which starts tipping as different sections grow at different rates.

Park Keeper: "See how it's tilting? In real life, your equity funds might grow faster than your debt funds, pushing your allocation out of whack. Time to rebalance!"

Kumar shifts his position, bringing the seesaw back to level.

Park Keeper: "Great job! In your portfolio, you'd sell some of the assets that have grown too much and buy more of those that have lagged. This keeps your risk level consistent and can even boost returns!"

Lesson: Regular rebalancing helps maintain your desired asset allocation and can improve long-term performance.

Scene 4: The Goal-Based Treasure Hunt

Kumar joins a treasure hunt where each chest represents a financial goal.

Hunt Master: "Each treasure chest needs a different strategy to unlock. Just like your different financial goals!"

Kumar finds chests labeled:

1. "Emergency Fund" (opens easily)
2. "Down Payment for House" (requires a bit more effort)
3. "Child's Education" (needs long-term planning)
4. "Retirement" (the most challenging to unlock)

Hunt Master: "For short-term goals, focus on safer, more liquid funds. For long-term goals, you can afford to take more risk for potentially higher returns."

Lesson: Align your mutual fund choices with your specific financial goals and their time horizons.

Scene 5: The SIP Waterfall

Kumar reaches a beautiful waterfall with a steady flow of water.

Waterfall Guide: "This is the SIP Waterfall! Notice how the steady flow of water has carved out this magnificent landscape over time?"

Kumar: "It's breathtaking! But what does this have to do with mutual funds?"

Waterfall Guide: "Everything! This represents the power of Systematic Investment Plans (SIPs). By investing a fixed amount regularly, you can build substantial wealth over time, regardless of market ups and downs."

The guide shows Kumar a simulation of how small, regular investments can grow into a substantial sum over years.

Lesson: SIPs can help you build wealth steadily and take advantage of market fluctuations through rupee cost averaging.

Climax: The Portfolio Management Palace

Finally, Kumar reaches a grand palace where all his experiences come together.

Palace Keeper: "Welcome to the Portfolio Management Palace! Here's where you use everything you've learned to create and manage your perfect portfolio."

Kumar uses his knowledge of asset allocation, diversification, rebalancing, goal-based investing, and SIPs to navigate through the palace, creating a portfolio that's just right for him.

Palace Keeper: "Remember, Kumar, the perfect portfolio isn't about maximizing returns at all costs. It's about creating a mix that helps you sleep well at night and achieve your financial goals."

Final Lesson: Building the perfect portfolio is a personal journey. It involves understanding your goals, choosing the right mix of funds, and regularly reviewing and adjusting your investments.

And cut! That's a wrap on "Mutual Fund Masala 4: The Quest for the Perfect Portfolio". Remember, dear viewers, in the world of mutual funds, the real treasure is a well-planned, diversified portfolio that aligns with your goals!

As the credits roll, we see Mutual Kumar confidently managing his portfolio, ready for whatever financial adventures life brings next!

Mutual Fund Masala: The Great Indian Savings Race

Lights, camera, action! Welcome to a special edition of our mutual fund blockbuster series. In this thrilling event, we witness an epic race between different savings methods. Get ready for "The Great Indian Savings Race"!

Scene 1: The Starting Line

We open at a colorful racing track. Contestants are lining up at the starting line, each representing a different savings method.

Race Announcer: "Ladies and gentlemen, welcome to The Great Indian Savings Race! Let's meet our contestants!"

1. Fixed Deposit Feroz: A sturdy, reliable-looking fellow in a bankers' suit.
2. Savings Account Savita: A friendly lady with a piggy bank in hand.
3. Mutual Fund Meena: A dynamic woman in sports gear, ready to run.
4. Gold Gujarmal: A glittering character, weighed down by gold chains.
5. Real Estate Rakesh: A man carrying a tiny house on his back.

Mutual Kumar: "Wow! Who do you think will win?"

Race Announcer: "That depends on the track and the duration, Kumar. Let's see how they perform!"

Lesson: Different savings methods have different characteristics and perform differently over various time periods.

Scene 2: The Short Sprint (1-3 years)

The whistle blows, and the racers take off for a short sprint.

Race Announcer: "And they're off! For this short race, safety and liquidity are key!"

Fixed Deposit Feroz takes an early lead, with Savings Account Savita close behind. Mutual Fund Meena struggles with some hurdles (market volatility), while Gold Gujarmal and Real Estate Rakesh barely move.

Race Announcer: "For short-term goals, Fixed Deposits and Savings Accounts often shine due to their stability and easy access to funds!"

Lesson: For short-term savings, traditional methods like FDs and savings accounts can be suitable due to their safety and liquidity.

Scene 3: The Middle Distance (3-7 years)

The race continues into the middle distance section.

Race Announcer: "As we enter the middle distance, we need a balance of growth and stability!"

Mutual Fund Meena starts to pick up pace, overtaking Fixed Deposit Feroz. Gold Gujarmal gains some ground, while Real Estate Rakesh still struggles to get moving.

Race Announcer: "In the medium term, Mutual Funds, especially balanced funds, can potentially offer better returns than traditional savings methods, while managing risk!"

Lesson: For medium-term goals, mutual funds can offer a good balance of returns and risk management.

Scene 4: The Long Haul (7+ years)

The race enters its final, longest stretch.

Race Announcer: "Now we're in for the long haul! This is where wealth creation happens!"

Mutual Fund Meena surges ahead, leaving Fixed Deposit Feroz and Savings Account Savita far behind. Gold Gujarmal maintains a steady pace, while Real Estate Rakesh finally gets moving and starts to catch up.

Race Announcer: "In the long run, Mutual Funds, especially equity funds, have the potential to significantly outperform traditional savings methods!"

Lesson: For long-term wealth creation, mutual funds, particularly equity funds, have historically offered higher returns compared to traditional savings methods.

Scene 5: The Inflation Hurdles

Throughout the race, all contestants face hurdles labeled "Inflation".

Race Announcer: "Oh no! Inflation hurdles! Let's see how our contestants handle them!"

Fixed Deposit Feroz and Savings Account Savita struggle to clear these hurdles, often hitting them. Mutual Fund Meena clears most hurdles with ease. Gold Gujarmal and Real Estate Rakesh clear some, but stumble on others.

Race Announcer: "Inflation can erode the value of your savings over time. It's crucial to choose a savings method that has the potential to beat inflation!"

Lesson: Mutual funds, especially equity funds, have the potential to offer inflation-beating returns over the long term, unlike many traditional savings methods.

Scene 6: The Tax Trap

Near the finish line, contestants face a "Tax Trap".

Race Announcer: "Watch out for the Tax Trap! This can significantly impact your final returns!"

Fixed Deposit Feroz gets caught in the trap, slowing down significantly. Mutual Fund Meena navigates it more easily, especially in the equity lane.

Race Announcer: "Some mutual funds, like ELSS, offer tax benefits that traditional savings methods don't. Always consider the post-tax returns!"

Lesson: Consider the tax implications of different savings methods. Some mutual funds offer tax advantages over traditional savings options.

Climax: The Finish Line

As the contestants cross the finish line, we see a split screen showing their performance over different race durations.

Race Announcer: "And there you have it, folks! While Fixed Deposit Feroz and Savings Account Savita led in the short sprint, Mutual Fund Meena dominated the long haul. Gold Gujarmal and Real Estate Rakesh had their moments too!"

Mutual Kumar: "So, there's no one clear winner for all situations?"

Race Announcer: "Exactly, Kumar! The best savings method depends on your financial goals, time horizon, and risk tolerance. Often, a combination works best!"

Final Lesson: While mutual funds have the potential to offer higher returns, especially over the long term, traditional savings methods have their place too. The key is to choose the right tool for your financial goals.

And cut! That's a wrap on "The Great Indian Savings Race"! Remember, dear viewers, in the world of savings and investments, it's not about finding a single winner, but about creating a winning combination that works for you!

As the credits roll, we see Mutual Kumar thoughtfully planning his savings strategy, allocating his money across different methods based on his goals and timelines.

3

Stocks vs. Mutual Funds: The Daal and Roti of Indian Investing

Investing Essentials: Daal & Roti Explained

Lights, camera, action! Welcome to "Master Chef Investor," the show where we cook up delicious investment recipes! Today, we're comparing two staples of the Indian financial diet: Stocks and Mutual Funds. Get ready to tantalize your taste buds and your wallet!

Scene 1: The Kitchen Introduction

We open in a bustling kitchen. Our host, Chef Mutual Kumar, stands at the counter with two plates: one with individual ingredients, another with a ready-made thali.

Chef Kumar: "Namaste, food lovers and money makers! Today, we're cooking up a financial feast. On my right, we have individual ingredients for our dish - that's like buying stocks. On my left, we have a ready-made thali - that's similar to investing in mutual funds. Let's dig in!"

Lesson: Stocks are like individual ingredients you choose yourself, while mutual funds are pre-prepared meals (portfolios) made by professional chefs (fund managers).

Scene 2: The Recipe (How They Work)

Chef Kumar moves to the cooking station.

Chef Kumar: "When you buy stocks, you're buying a small piece of a company, like buying a pinch of masala. With mutual funds, you're buying a portion of a pre-made dish that contains many ingredients (stocks) chosen and mixed by an expert chef (fund manager)."

He starts cooking, carefully measuring individual spices for one dish (stocks), while quickly heating a pre-made curry (mutual funds) for another.

Chef Kumar: "See how I need to carefully choose each ingredient for the stock dish? It takes time and knowledge. But for the mutual fund dish, I'm relying on a pre-made mix created by an expert."

Lesson: Investing in stocks requires more individual research and decision-making, while mutual funds offer professional management and built-in diversification.

Scene 3: The Taste Test (Returns)

Two food critics arrive to taste the dishes.

Critic 1 (tasting the stock dish): "Wow! This particular masala (stock) is amazing! But... this other one is a bit off."

Critic 2 (tasting the mutual fund dish): "Hmm, it's good overall. Not exceptional in any one flavor, but satisfying and well-balanced."

Chef Kumar: "Just like our dishes, stocks can give you exceptional returns if you pick the right ones, but they're riskier. Mutual funds generally give steadier, more balanced returns."

Lesson: Stocks have the potential for higher returns (and losses) on individual picks, while mutual funds offer more consistent, diversified returns.

Scene 4: The Kitchen Chaos (Risk Management)

Suddenly, there's a power cut in the kitchen. Chef Kumar calmly continues with the mutual fund dish but struggles with the individual stock ingredients in the dark.

Chef Kumar: "Oh no! See how it's harder to manage all these individual ingredients in a crisis? But our pre-made mutual fund dish is still okay. This is like how mutual funds can help manage risk through diversification."

Lesson: Mutual funds inherently offer risk management through diversification, while managing risk with individual stocks requires more active management.

Scene 5: The Budget (Minimum Investment)

A young apprentice chef approaches, looking to learn.

Apprentice: "Chef, I want to start cooking, but I don't have much money for ingredients."

Chef Kumar: "Ah! For our stock dish, you'd need to buy each ingredient separately, which can be costly. But for our mutual fund dish, you can start with just a small portion. Some mutual funds let you start with as little as ₹500!"

Lesson: Mutual funds often have lower minimum investment requirements compared to creating a diversified stock portfolio yourself.

Scene 6: The Cooking Time (Time and Effort)

We see a time-lapse of Chef Kumar constantly checking and adjusting the stock dish, while the mutual fund dish simmers quietly with occasional stirring.

Chef Kumar: "Notice how the stock dish needs constant attention? That's like monitoring and managing your stock investments. The mutual fund dish needs some attention, but much less – the fund manager does most of the work."

Lesson: Managing a stock portfolio typically requires more time and effort than investing in mutual funds.

Scene 7: The Masala Mix (Diversification)

Chef Kumar shows a spice box with many compartments.

Chef Kumar: "In stocks, you need to create your own spice mix, choosing each ingredient carefully. It's great if you know what you're doing, but it's easy to over-season! Mutual funds are like getting a premixed masala - diversification is built-in."

Lesson: Mutual funds offer instant diversification, while achieving the same with individual stocks requires more knowledge and capital.

Climax: The Grand Buffet

The kitchen transforms into a grand buffet, showcasing various stock dishes and mutual fund thalis.

Chef Kumar: "And here's our grand finale! Some expert chefs might create amazing individual dishes (stock picks), while others prefer the balanced meal of a thali (mutual funds). Many great investors use both!"

He turns to the camera with a warm smile.

Chef Kumar: "Remember, in the kitchen of investing, there's no one perfect recipe. Stocks and mutual funds are both important parts of a balanced financial diet. The best meal is the one that satisfies your taste (goals), suits your spice tolerance (risk appetite), and fits your budget!"

Final Lesson: Both stocks and mutual funds have their place in an investment portfolio. The right choice depends on your financial goals, risk tolerance, available time, and investing knowledge.

And cut! That's a wrap on "Stocks vs. Mutual Funds: The Daal and Roti of Indian Investing"! Remember, dear viewers, in the world of investments, the key to a satisfying financial meal is understanding your ingredients and creating a balanced diet!

As the credits roll, we see Mutual Kumar happily cooking up a storm, mixing individual stock ingredients with mutual fund dishes, creating his perfect investment menu.

4

The Great Indian Mutual Fund Bazaar: Types for Every Taste

Mutual Fund Mela: Explore Your Investment Palette

THE GREAT INDIAN MUTUAL FUND BAZAAR: TYPES FOR EVERY TASTE

Lights, camera, action! Welcome to "The Great Indian Mutual Fund Bazaar," where we'll explore the colorful world of mutual fund types available in India. Join our hero, Mutual Kumar, as he navigates this bustling financial marketplace!

Scene 1: Entering the Bazaar

Mutual Kumar approaches a vibrant, noisy bazaar with countless stalls and shops.

Bazaar Guide: "Welcome to The Great Indian Mutual Fund Bazaar, Kumar! Here, you'll find a mutual fund for every taste and need. Let's explore!"

Kumar: "Wow! There's so much variety. Where do we start?"

Bazaar Guide: "Let's begin with the most popular sections. Remember, each shop represents a different type of mutual fund!"

Lesson: The Indian mutual fund market offers a wide variety of fund types to suit different investment needs and preferences.

Scene 2: Equity Street

They turn into a busy street lined with shops selling stocks.

Bazaar Guide: "This is Equity Street, where funds primarily invest in stocks. Let's check out some shops!"

1. Large-Cap Lassi Stand Shopkeeper: "Our large-cap fund is like a refreshing lassi - cool, reliable, and satisfying!" Example: "Try our bestseller - HDFC Top 100 Fund. It's like the King of Good Times in the large-cap world!"
2. Mid-Cap Masala Dosa Corner Shopkeeper: "Mid-cap funds are like masala dosas - spicier and more exciting, with

potential for great taste!" Example: "Sample our Kotak Emerging Equity Fund - it's been serving up delicious returns!"

3. Small-Cap Golgappa Stall Shopkeeper: "Small-cap funds are like golgappas - small, explosive bursts of flavor, but not for the faint-hearted!" Example: "Try our Nippon India Small Cap Fund - it's been the talk of the town!"

Kumar: "These all sound tempting, but also a bit risky."

Bazaar Guide: "You're right! Equity funds can be volatile, but they also offer potential for high returns over the long term."

Lesson: Equity funds invest primarily in stocks and are categorized based on the size of companies they invest in. They offer high growth potential but come with higher risk.

Scene 3: Debt Boulevard

They move to a quieter, more orderly street.

Bazaar Guide: "Welcome to Debt Boulevard. Here, funds deal with fixed-income securities. It's less exciting, but steadier."

1. Government Securities Ghee Shop Shopkeeper: "Our funds are like pure ghee - safe, essential, and good for long-term financial health!" Example: "SBI Magnum Gilt Fund is our premium offering - as reliable as the government itself!"

2. Corporate Bond Chai Stall Shopkeeper: "Corporate bond funds are like a good cup of chai - familiar, comforting, with a bit more flavor than plain milk!" Example: "ICICI Prudential Corporate Bond Fund - a balanced blend for your portfolio!"

3. Liquid Funds Nimbu Pani Stand Shopkeeper: "Liquid funds

are like refreshing nimbu pani - quick, easy, and perfect for short-term needs!" Example: "Aditya Birla Sun Life Liquid Fund - when you need your money as quickly as you drink nimbu pani!"

Kumar: "These seem less risky than the equity funds."

Bazaar Guide: "Exactly! Debt funds are generally more stable but offer lower returns compared to equity funds."

Lesson: Debt funds invest in fixed-income securities and are generally less risky than equity funds. They're suitable for conservative investors or for short-term goals.

Scene 4: Hybrid Haveli

They approach a grand haveli in the center of the bazaar.

Bazaar Guide: "This is the Hybrid Haveli, where funds mix equity and debt in different proportions."

1. Balanced Funds Balcony Shopkeeper: "Our balanced funds are like a perfect thali - a bit of everything for a satisfying meal!" Example: "ICICI Prudential Balanced Advantage Fund - adjusts its equity-debt mix based on market conditions, like a chef adjusting spices!"
2. Aggressive Hybrid Funds Andhra Mess Shopkeeper: "More spice, more equity! For those who like their portfolio hot!" Example: "Mirae Asset Hybrid Equity Fund - a spicy mix with a bigger portion of equity!"

Kumar: "This seems like a good middle ground between equity and debt."

Bazaar Guide: "Exactly! Hybrid funds try to offer the best of both worlds."

Lesson: Hybrid funds mix equity and debt in various proportions, offering a balance between growth and stability.

Scene 5: The Index Imitation Alley

They walk down a street where all shops look identical.

Bazaar Guide: "This is Index Imitation Alley. These funds don't try to beat the market, they simply mimic it!"

1. Nifty Fifty Naan Shop Shopkeeper: "We recreate the Nifty 50 index, just like how we faithfully recreate your favorite naan!" Example: "UTI Nifty Index Fund - it rises and falls with the Nifty, no surprises!"
2. Sensex Samosa Stall Shopkeeper: "Our fund is shaped exactly like the Sensex, just like our perfectly shaped samosas!" Example: "HDFC Index Fund - Sensex Plan. It's the Sensex in a mutual fund wrapper!"

Kumar: "So these don't try to outsmart the market?"

Bazaar Guide: "Nope! They aim to match the market's performance, usually with lower fees."

Lesson: Index funds aim to replicate the performance of a specific market index, offering market returns at lower costs.

Scene 6: Sectoral Specialties Square

They enter a square with shops representing different industries.

Bazaar Guide: "Here we have Sectoral Funds, each focusing on a specific industry."

1. Tech Tadka Shop Shopkeeper: "We add a tech tadka to your portfolio!" Example: "ICICI Prudential Technology Fund - riding the IT wave!"
2. Pharma Pani Puri Stall Shopkeeper: "Health is wealth, and so is our pharma fund!" Example: "Nippon India Pharma Fund - a booster dose for your investments!"

Kumar: "These seem very focused."

Bazaar Guide: "Yes, they can offer high returns but are also riskier due to lack of diversification."

Lesson: Sectoral funds focus on specific industries, offering high growth potential but with increased risk.

Climax: The Fund of Funds Food Court

They end up at a grand food court representing Fund of Funds.

Bazaar Guide: "And finally, we have the Fund of Funds Food Court. These funds invest in other mutual funds, offering you a buffet of investment options!"

Example: "Franklin India Dynamic Asset Allocation Fund of Funds - it's like having a personal chef create a perfect meal from the best dishes in the bazaar!"

Kumar: "This bazaar is amazing! So many options to choose from."

Bazaar Guide: "Indeed! The key is to choose the funds that match your taste (financial goals), spice tolerance (risk appetite), and dietary restrictions (investment constraints)."

Final Lesson: The Indian mutual fund market offers a wide variety of options. The key is to understand each type and choose funds that align with your financial goals and risk tolerance.

And cut! That's a wrap on "The Great Indian Mutual Fund

Bazaar"! Remember, dear viewers, in this financial bazaar, the best shopping experience comes from understanding what you're buying and why it fits your needs!

As the credits roll, we see Mutual Kumar excitedly planning his mutual fund portfolio, mixing and matching different types of funds like a seasoned bazaar shopper.

5

Tech Tadka: The Spice of Modern Mutual Fund Investing

Tech Tadka: Spicing Up Modern Mutual Fund Investing

Lights, camera, action! Welcome to "Tech Tadka: The Spice

of Modern Mutual Fund Investing," where we explore how technology is spicing up the world of mutual funds in India. Join our hero, Mutual Kumar, as he navigates the dazzling Tech Tadka Expo 2023!

Scene 1: Entering the Tech Tadka Expo

Mutual Kumar approaches a futuristic expo center with holographic displays and neon lights.

Tech Guide: "Welcome to the Tech Tadka Expo 2023, Kumar! Here, we showcase how technology is revolutionizing mutual fund investing in India. Ready to add some tech tadka to your financial diet?"

Kumar: "Absolutely! But I'm not very tech-savvy. Will I be able to understand all this?"

Tech Guide: "Don't worry! These tech solutions are designed to make investing easier, not more complicated. Let's dive in!"

Lesson: Modern mutual fund technologies aim to simplify investing, making it accessible to everyone, regardless of their tech expertise.

Scene 2: The Mobile App Mela

They enter a vibrant section filled with giant smartphone replicas.

Tech Guide: "Welcome to the Mobile App Mela! Here, you can explore popular mutual fund apps that put the power of investing in your pocket."

1. Groww Golgappa Stall Demo Host: "Try our Groww app - it's as easy to use as eating golgappas! You can invest in

TECH TADKA: THE SPICE OF MODERN MUTUAL FUND INVESTING

mutual funds with just a few taps." Kumar tries the app: "Wow! I can see fund performance, set up SIPs, and even track my investments all in one place!"
2. Zerodha Coin Zest Corner Demo Host: "Zerodha Coin is like adding zesty lemon to your investment recipe. Direct mutual funds with zero commission!" Kumar explores: "I like how it integrates with my trading account. And look at these detailed fund analyses!"
3. ET Money Masala Mix Demo Host: "ET Money is your all-in-one financial masala mix! Mutual funds, insurance, and even tax saving in one app." Kumar tests it: "The goal-based investing feature is really helpful. It's like having a financial advisor in my pocket!"

Tech Guide: "These apps have made mutual fund investing as easy as ordering food online. No more paperwork or visiting branch offices!"

Lesson: Mobile apps have revolutionized mutual fund investing, offering convenience, detailed information, and easy transaction processes.

Scene 3: The Robo-Advisor Raj

They move to a section with sleek robots dressed as financial advisors.

Tech Guide: "Welcome to the Robo-Advisor Raj! These AI-powered platforms offer automated, algorithm-based fund selection and portfolio management."

1. Scripbox Samosa Server Robo-Advisor: "Hello! I analyze your financial goals and risk tolerance to serve up a perfect

samosa platter of mutual funds." Kumar interacts: "It's asking me questions about my income, goals, and risk appetite. Oh, and now it's recommending a portfolio!"

2. Kuvera Kheer Kiosk Robo-Advisor: "I'm here to make your investment journey as smooth as kheer! I'll even help you consolidate all your mutual fund investments." Kumar tries it: "I like how it's showing me the tax implications of my investment choices. Very helpful!"

Tech Guide: "Robo-advisors use complex algorithms to offer personalized investment advice at a fraction of the cost of human advisors."

Lesson: Robo-advisors provide automated, personalized investment advice and portfolio management, making professional-grade investing accessible to all.

Scene 4: The Digital KYC Dhaba

They approach a stall with a giant Aadhaar card display.

Tech Guide: "This is the Digital KYC Dhaba, where opening a mutual fund account is as easy as making instant noodles!"

Demo Host: "Gone are the days of lengthy paperwork. With e-KYC, you can start investing in minutes! All you need is your Aadhaar and PAN."

Kumar tries it out: "This is incredible! I just entered my Aadhaar number, did a quick biometric verification, and my KYC is done!"

Tech Guide: "Digital KYC has made the account opening process super fast and convenient. It's one of the biggest tech leaps in Indian mutual funds."

Lesson: Digital KYC has significantly simplified the process of starting mutual fund investments, reducing paperwork and time required.

Scene 5: The SIP Automation Station

They visit a stall with robots making regular, rhythmic movements.

Tech Guide: "Welcome to the SIP Automation Station! Here, technology ensures your investments keep flowing like a smooth, steady stream."

Demo Host: "With automated SIPs, you can set up regular investments that happen automatically. No need to remember dates or make manual transfers!"

Kumar explores: "I can set up monthly, quarterly, or even weekly SIPs. And look, I can even increase my SIP amount automatically each year!"

Tech Guide: "SIP automation ensures disciplined investing. It's like setting up a recurring digital piggy bank!"

Lesson: Automated SIPs leverage technology to ensure regular, disciplined investing without manual intervention.

Scene 6: The Analytics Adda

They enter a section with giant, interactive charts and graphs.

Tech Guide: "This is the Analytics Adda, where data becomes your best friend in making investment decisions."

1. CAMS Online Chai Shop Demo Host: "Just like a good cup of chai, we brew up all your mutual fund data across different AMCs into one consolidated view." Kumar tries it: "I can see my entire mutual fund portfolio, even if I've invested

through different platforms!"
2. MFCentral Masala Mixer Demo Host: "We're the one-stop-shop for all your mutual fund needs - from viewing your portfolio to initiating transactions." Kumar explores: "This is great! I can even raise service requests and complaints for all my funds in one place."

Tech Guide: "These platforms offer deep insights into your investments, helping you make data-driven decisions."

Lesson: Advanced analytics tools provide investors with comprehensive insights into their mutual fund portfolios, aiding in better decision-making.

Climax: The Virtual Reality Investing Theater

For the grand finale, they enter a futuristic theater with VR headsets.

Tech Guide: "And now, for a glimpse into the future of mutual fund investing!"

Kumar puts on a VR headset and finds himself in a virtual financial world where he can interact with fund managers, visualize market trends in 3D, and even 'walk through' the companies he's investing in.

Kumar (amazed): "This is incredible! I feel like I truly understand where my money is going!"

Tech Guide: "While this level of VR isn't widely available yet, it shows how technology might shape the future of investing. Imagine learning about mutual funds through immersive experiences!"

Final Lesson: Technology continues to evolve, promising even more intuitive and immersive ways to understand and engage with mutual fund investments in the future.

And cut! That's a wrap on "Tech Tadka: The Spice of Modern Mutual Fund Investing"! Remember, dear viewers, in this digital age, technology is your secret ingredient for a flavorful and successful mutual fund investment journey!

As the credits roll, we see Mutual Kumar excitedly downloading various mutual fund apps on his smartphone, ready to embark on his tech-savvy investment adventure.

6

Choosing Your Perfect Mutual Fund: Like Finding Your Favorite Street Food

Finding Your Flavor: Navigating Mutual Funds Like Street Food

Lights, camera, action! Welcome to "The Great Indian Fund

Feast," where choosing a mutual fund is as exciting as exploring a street food festival! Join our hero, Mutual Kumar, as he navigates the bustling lanes of financial flavors!

Scene 1: Entering the Fund Feast

Mutual Kumar approaches a vibrant street food festival with countless stalls, each representing a different mutual fund.

Food Guide: "Welcome to The Great Indian Fund Feast, Kumar! Here, we'll help you find the perfect mutual fund that suits your financial palate. Ready to taste some financial flavors?"

Kumar: "Absolutely! But how do I choose? There are so many options!"

Food Guide: "Just like choosing street food, picking a mutual fund is about knowing your taste, your hunger level, and your spice tolerance. Let's explore!"

Lesson: Choosing a mutual fund, like selecting street food, is a personal decision based on individual preferences and needs.

Scene 2: The Risk Appetite Meter

They approach a stall with a giant "Risk-o-meter" display, resembling a spice level indicator.

Food Guide: "Before we start tasting, let's measure your risk appetite. It's like determining your spice tolerance!"

Kumar tries the Risk-o-meter, which asks questions about his comfort with market fluctuations and potential losses.

Risk-o-meter Host: "Based on your responses, your risk appetite is 'Medium'. You can handle some spice, but you're not ready for the ghost pepper of high-risk funds!"

Food Guide: "Great! Now we know to look for funds that match your medium risk tolerance. This could mean a mix of equity and debt funds."

Lesson: Understanding your risk appetite is crucial in selecting appropriate mutual funds, just as knowing your spice tolerance helps in choosing the right street food.

Scene 3: The Financial Goals Thali

They move to a stall offering various thalis, each representing different financial goals.

Food Guide: "Now, let's identify your financial goals. It's like choosing between a quick snack, a full meal, or a feast for a special occasion."

Kumar looks at the options:

1. Short-term Snack Thali (0-3 years): For quick financial needs
2. Medium-term Meal Thali (3-7 years): For intermediate financial goals
3. Long-term Feast Thali (7+ years): For long-term wealth creation

Kumar: "I'm saving for a house down payment in 5 years, and also for retirement in the long term."

Food Guide: "Excellent! So we'll look for a mix of medium-term and long-term funds. It's like crafting a balanced meal with different courses."

Lesson: Aligning your mutual fund choices with your financial goals and their time horizons is essential for effective investing.

Scene 4: The Return Expectation Juice Bar

They visit a colorful juice stall with various fruits representing different return potentials.

Juice Bartender: "What's your return expectation flavor, sir? We have Conservative Coconut Water, Balanced Mixed Fruit Juice, and Aggressive Exotic Smoothie!"

Kumar: "I'd like something balanced but with a chance for higher returns."

Juice Bartender serves a Mixed Fruit Juice with a dash of exotic fruits.

Food Guide: "Remember, Kumar, higher return potential often comes with higher risk. It's like adding spicier ingredients to your juice – exciting, but not for everyone!"

Lesson: Return expectations should be realistic and aligned with your risk appetite. Higher returns typically involve higher risks.

Scene 5: The Diversification Chaat Corner

They approach a chaat stall with a variety of ingredients.

Food Guide: "Diversification in mutual funds is like making the perfect chaat. You need a mix of ingredients to balance flavors and reduce the risk of any one ingredient spoiling the dish."

Chaat Maker: "Let me make you a diversified chaat plate! We'll mix some equity funds (spicy puri), debt funds (cooling dahi), and maybe a dash of international funds (exotic pomegranate seeds)."

Kumar tastes the diversified chaat: "Wow! It's a perfect blend of flavors!"

Lesson: Diversification helps balance risk and return in your mutual fund portfolio, just as a variety of ingredients creates a balanced and delightful chaat.

Scene 6: The Fund Manager's Kitchen

They peek into an open kitchen where skilled chefs (fund managers) are at work.

Food Guide: "The fund manager's track record is like a chef's reputation. Let's check out their past performances and cooking style!"

They watch different chefs:

1. Chef Consistent: Known for steady, reliable performances
2. Chef High-Risk High-Reward: Famous for spectacular successes (and some failures)
3. Chef Newcomer: Promising but unproven

Kumar: "I think I prefer Chef Consistent for my main course, but maybe I'll try a small dish from Chef High-Risk for that extra flavor!"

Lesson: A fund manager's track record and investment style are important factors to consider when choosing mutual funds.

Scene 7: The Expense Ratio Weighing Scale

They stop at a stall with a large weighing scale.

Food Guide: "Before you finalize your choice, always check the expense ratio. It's like weighing your street food – you want good value for money!"

Kumar places different fund options on the scale, seeing how their expense ratios compare.

Scale Operator: "Remember, a lower expense ratio means more of your returns stay in your pocket. But sometimes, paying a bit extra for a really good fund can be worth it!"

Lesson: The expense ratio impacts your overall returns. While lower is generally better, it shouldn't be the only factor in your decision.

Climax: Crafting Your Perfect Financial Menu

As they reach the end of the festival, Kumar sits down with his Food Guide to plan his mutual fund 'menu'.

Food Guide: "Now that we've explored all the flavors, let's craft your perfect mutual fund menu!"

Kumar: "I think I'll start with a large portion of that balanced equity fund for my long-term goals, a side of debt fund for stability, and a small taste of that high-risk sectoral fund for potential extra returns."

Food Guide: "Excellent choices! And remember, just like your taste in food might change over time, your financial menu should be reviewed and adjusted periodically."

Final Lesson: Choosing mutual funds is a personal journey based on your risk appetite, financial goals, return expectations, and need for diversification. Regular review and rebalancing are key to maintaining a healthy financial diet.

And cut! That's a wrap on "Choosing Your Perfect Mutual Fund: Like Finding Your Favorite Street Food"! Remember, dear viewers, in the grand street food festival of mutual funds, the perfect meal is one that satisfies your financial hunger without giving you indigestion!

As the credits roll, we see Mutual Kumar confidently crafting his mutual fund portfolio, mixing and matching funds like a seasoned street food connoisseur.

7

The Art of Investing: Timing Your Entry Like a Mumbai Local

Investing in Motion: Leap into the Market

Lights, camera, action! Welcome to "The Mumbai Local Investment Express," where timing your mutual fund investments is as thrilling as catching a Mumbai local train! Join our hero, Mutual Kumar, as he navigates the bustling financial railways of Mumbai!

Scene 1: Entering Churchgate Station

Mutual Kumar enters the busy Churchgate station, looking overwhelmed by the crowds and trains.

Train Guide: "Welcome to the Mumbai Local Investment Express, Kumar! Here, we'll learn how to time our mutual fund investments like a pro Mumbaikar catches trains. Ready for a financial ride?"

Kumar: "Absolutely! But it looks so chaotic. How do I know when to jump in?"

Train Guide: "That's the art we'll master today. Let's start our journey!"

Lesson: Timing investments in mutual funds can seem overwhelming, but with the right strategies, it can be mastered.

Scene 2: The Lump Sum Express

They approach a relatively empty platform with a luxurious-looking train.

Train Guide: "This is the Lump Sum Express. It's like booking an entire coach for yourself – you invest a large amount at once."

Kumar: "Wow, that looks comfortable! But what if I board at the wrong time?"

Train Guide: "Exactly! Timing is crucial here. If you catch it at a market low, you could get a smooth, profitable ride. But if you board at a peak, you might face a bumpy journey."

A group of passengers rush to board as the market news ticker shows "Markets at All-Time High!"

Train Guide: "See? They might be jumping in at the wrong time. Lump sum investments work best when markets are low or you have insider knowledge of a station that's about to become popular."

Lesson: Lump sum investments can be powerful but timing is critical. They're best suited when you believe the market is undervalued.

Scene 3: The SIP Local Train

They move to a platform with a train that arrives at regular intervals.

Train Guide: "This is the SIP Local – the Systematic Investment Plan train. It's the most popular route for regular commuters in the investment world."

Kumar watches as passengers board the train in an orderly fashion at each stop.

Train Guide: "With SIP, you invest a fixed amount regularly, regardless of market conditions. It's like boarding the train at the same time every day, whether it's crowded or empty."

Kumar: "But what if the train is too crowded one day?"

Train Guide: "That's the beauty of it! On crowded days (high market prices), your fixed amount buys fewer units. On empty days (low market prices), you get more units. Over time, this averages out your purchase cost."

Lesson: SIP is a disciplined investment approach that takes advantage of market fluctuations through rupee-cost averaging.

Scene 4: The Rupee-Cost Averaging Junction

They reach a special junction where trains from different lines converge.

Train Guide: "Welcome to Rupee-Cost Averaging Junction! This is where the magic of SIP happens."

They watch a demonstration:

- In January, ₹1000 buys 50 units at ₹20 per unit
- In February, ₹1000 buys 40 units at ₹25 per unit
- In March, ₹1000 buys 67 units at ₹15 per unit

Train Guide: "See? You've invested ₹3000 in total and got 157 units. Your average cost per unit is ₹19.11, even though the actual price fluctuated between ₹15 and ₹25!"

Kumar: "That's brilliant! It's like getting a discount on some days to offset the expensive days."

Lesson: Rupee-cost averaging (the Indian version of dollar-cost averaging) helps in reducing the impact of market volatility on your investments.

Scene 5: The Value Averaging Fast Local

They approach a platform with a sleek, fast train.

Train Guide: "This is for more advanced travelers – the Value Averaging Fast Local. Here, you adjust your investment amount based on market performance."

They watch as passengers put in varying amounts at each stop:

- When the market is down, they invest more
- When the market is up, they invest less

Train Guide: "It's like adding more coaches to the train when tickets are cheap, and reducing them when they're expensive."

Kumar: "Sounds effective, but it seems to require more attention and flexibility with my budget."

Train Guide: "Exactly! It can be very effective but needs more active management."

Lesson: Value averaging can potentially enhance returns but requires more effort and financial flexibility.

Scene 6: The Market Timing Express

They see a group of anxious-looking passengers constantly checking their watches and market updates on their phones.

Train Guide: "Those folks are trying to catch the Market Timing Express. They're attempting to perfectly time the market bottoms and peaks."

They watch as some passengers miss the train waiting for the "perfect" moment, while others jump on and off frantically.

Kumar: "That looks stressful and risky!"

Train Guide: "It is! Even financial experts often fail at consistent market timing. For most investors, it's better to focus on 'time in the market' rather than 'timing the market'."

Lesson: Trying to perfectly time the market is difficult and risky. Consistent, long-term investing often yields better results.

Scene 7: The Long-Term Investor's Duronto

They arrive at a platform with a train prepared for a long journey.

Train Guide: "This is the Long-Term Investor's Duronto. It's for passengers who are in for the long haul, not worried about short-term station stops."

Kumar watches as relaxed passengers board with books and comfortable pillows.

Train Guide: "These investors understand that over long periods, the journey tends to be upward, despite short-term bumps. They focus on the destination, not every small station in between."

Lesson: Long-term investing in mutual funds can help overcome short-term market volatility and potentially yield better returns.

Climax: Choosing Your Investment Route

As they reach the main concourse, Kumar sees boards displaying different investment routes.

Train Guide: "Now that you've seen all the options, which train will you choose for your investment journey?"

Kumar: "I think I'll start with the SIP Local for my regular investments. It seems like a safe and steady way to build my portfolio. But I might occasionally hop onto the Lump Sum Express if I see a good opportunity!"

Train Guide: "Excellent choice! Remember, the best investment strategy is one that you can stick with consistently, through busy stations and empty ones."

Final Lesson: The key to successful mutual fund investing is choosing a strategy that aligns with your financial goals, risk tolerance, and personal circumstances – and sticking to it consistently.

And cut! That's a wrap on "The Art of Investing: Timing Your Entry Like a Mumbai Local"! Remember, dear viewers, in the grand railway network of mutual fund investing, it's not just about catching the right train, but enjoying and staying committed to the entire journey!

As the credits roll, we see Mutual Kumar confidently planning his investment journey, mixing SIPs with occasional lump sum investments, ready to ride the Mumbai Local Investment Express to his financial destinations.

8

Navigating the Markets: Your GPS Through Bull and Bear Alleys

Market GPS: Navigating Bull & Bear Alleys

Lights, camera, action! Welcome to "The Great Indian Market Safari," where understanding market cycles is as thrilling as a road trip through a wildlife sanctuary! Join our hero, Mutual Kumar, as he navigates the wild terrains of the financial jungle!

Scene 1: Entering the Financial Forest

Mutual Kumar approaches a colorful Jeep with "Market Safari" painted on the side.

Safari Guide: "Welcome to The Great Indian Market Safari, Kumar! Today, we'll explore the natural habitat of bulls and bears, and see how they affect our mutual fund journey. Ready for an adventure?"

Kumar: "Absolutely! But I'm a bit nervous about encountering bears."

Safari Guide: "Don't worry! In this jungle, bears can be as important as bulls. Let's start our expedition!"

Lesson: Market cycles, like ecosystems, have different phases, each playing a crucial role in the overall financial environment.

Scene 2: The Bull Run Boulevard

They drive onto a wide, uphill road with a statue of a charging bull.

Safari Guide: "Welcome to Bull Run Boulevard! This is where the markets are on an upswing."

They watch as mutual fund NAVs (represented by colorful balloons) rise higher and higher.

Kumar: "Wow! Everything seems to be going up. Should we invest all our money now?"

Safari Guide: "Careful! While bull runs are exciting, they don't last forever. It's like a sugar rush - great while it lasts, but what goes up must come down."

They notice some overconfident tourists buying everything in sight at the "Peak Prices Gift Shop".

Safari Guide: "See those folks? In a bull market, everyone feels like a genius. But smart investors stay cautious even in good times."

Lesson: Bull markets can significantly boost mutual fund returns, especially for equity funds. However, they can also lead to overconfidence and overvaluation.

Scene 3: The Bear Cave Descent

The road suddenly dips, and they enter a dimly lit tunnel with a bear statue at the entrance.

Safari Guide: "Brace yourself, we're entering the Bear Cave Descent. This is where markets experience a downturn."

They watch as mutual fund NAV balloons start to deflate.

Kumar (panicking): "Oh no! Our balloons are shrinking! Should we sell everything?"

Safari Guide: "Hold on! Bear markets can be scary, but they're a natural part of the cycle. It's like winter - it feels gloomy, but it sets the stage for new growth."

They pass by a "Panic Selling Pit Stop" where frantic investors are rushing to sell.

Safari Guide: "Look at that chaos. In bear markets, fear takes over. But remember, this is often the best time for long-term investors to buy quality funds at a discount."

Lesson: Bear markets can negatively impact mutual fund returns in the short term, but they also create opportunities for long-term investors.

Scene 4: The Value Valley

They emerge from the tunnel into a lush valley filled with undervalued assets.

Safari Guide: "Welcome to Value Valley! This is where patient investors find hidden gems during market downturns."

They watch smart investors (represented by wise owls) carefully selecting premium mutual funds at discounted rates.

Kumar: "So, bear markets can be good for buyers?"

Safari Guide: "Exactly! It's like a clearance sale at your favorite store. Quality items at lower prices!"

Lesson: Market downturns can offer opportunities to invest in high-quality mutual funds at attractive valuations.

Scene 5: The Cyclical Roundabout

They approach a massive roundabout with exits to different sectors: IT Highway, Pharma Path, Banking Boulevard, etc.

Safari Guide: "This is the Cyclical Roundabout. Different sectors take turns leading the market."

They watch as traffic flows heavily towards IT Highway, then shifts to Pharma Path, then to Banking Boulevard.

Kumar: "It's like a merry-go-round of market favorites!"

Safari Guide: "Precisely! That's why diversification across sectors in your mutual fund portfolio is crucial. You never know which sector will take the lead next."

Lesson: Different sectors perform differently across market cycles. A well-diversified mutual fund portfolio can help balance these cyclical shifts.

Scene 6: The Volatility Rapids

They reach a turbulent river crossing with rapidly changing water levels.

Safari Guide: "Hold tight! We're crossing the Volatility Rapids. This represents short-term market fluctuations."

Their Jeep bounces up and down as they cross.

Kumar (dizzy): "I feel queasy! How do we handle this?"

Safari Guide: "Focus on the other shore, not the waves. In investing, that means keeping your eyes on your long-term goals, not daily market movements."

They see some tourists with "Short-Term Trader" t-shirts being tossed about violently, while "Long-Term Investor" rafts glide through more smoothly.

Lesson: Short-term volatility can be unsettling, but a long-term perspective helps navigate through these fluctuations in mutual fund performance.

Scene 7: The Economic Indicators Observatory

They reach a hilltop observatory with various gauges and meters.

Safari Guide: "This is the Economic Indicators Observatory. Smart investors use these tools to understand where we are in the market cycle."

They examine different indicators:

- GDP Growth Gauge
- Inflation Thermometer
- Interest Rate Barometer
- Employment Seismograph

Kumar: "These seem helpful in predicting market movements!"

Safari Guide: "They're useful guides, but remember, no one can predict markets with 100% accuracy. These indicators help us make informed decisions, not foolproof predictions."

Lesson: Economic indicators can provide insights into market cycles, but they should be used as guides rather than guarantees in mutual fund investing.

Climax: The All-Weather Portfolio Plains

They finally reach a vast, balanced ecosystem with a mix of all terrains they've encountered.

Safari Guide: "Welcome to the All-Weather Portfolio Plains! This is where smart investors create a balanced habitat that can thrive in any market climate."

They observe a harmonious blend of different mutual funds:

- Equity funds (represented by energetic gazelles) for growth
- Debt funds (represented by sturdy elephants) for stability
- Gold funds (represented by rare golden eagles) for hedge against uncertainty
- International funds (represented by exotic flamingos) for geographical diversification

Kumar: "I see! So a well-balanced portfolio can help navigate through different market cycles?"

Safari Guide: "Exactly! It's about creating an investment ecosystem that can adapt to changing market seasons."

Final Lesson: A well-diversified mutual fund portfolio, balanced across asset classes and sectors, can help investors navigate various market cycles more effectively.

And cut! That's a wrap on "Navigating the Markets: Your GPS Through Bull and Bear Alleys"! Remember, dear viewers, in the great safari of market investing, it's not about avoiding the bears or chasing the bulls, but about building a resilient portfolio that can thrive in any financial weather!

As the credits roll, we see Mutual Kumar confidently sketching out his all-weather portfolio, ready to navigate the wild and wonderful world of market cycles.

9

Tax Savings: The Sweet Chutney of Mutual Fund Investing

Chutney of Savings: Savoring Mutual Fund Benefits

Lights, camera, action! Welcome to "MasterChef: Tax Savings Edition," where we'll cook up some delicious tax-saving recipes with mutual funds! Join our hero, Mutual Kumar, as he learns to prepare the sweetest chutney in the financial kitchen - tax savings!

Scene 1: The Financial Cuisine Kitchen

Mutual Kumar enters a colorful kitchen set with "Tax Savings Tadka" written in bright lights.

Chef Tax-Saver: "Welcome to MasterChef: Tax Savings Edition, Kumar! Today, we'll whip up some mouth-watering tax-saving dishes with mutual funds. Ready to add some zing to your financial diet?"

Kumar: "Absolutely! But I always thought tax-saving was a bitter pill to swallow."

Chef Tax-Saver: "Not anymore! Let's start with our star recipe - the ELSS Eclair!"

Lesson: Tax-saving through mutual funds can be an enjoyable and rewarding aspect of financial planning.

Scene 2: Cooking the ELSS Eclair

Chef Tax-Saver brings out ingredients labeled "Equity," "Lock-in Period," and "Section 80C."

Chef: "Let's make our ELSS Eclair! ELSS stands for Equity Linked Savings Scheme. It's the dessert that satisfies both your sweet tooth and the taxman!"

Kumar starts mixing ingredients under the chef's guidance.

Chef: "We start with a base of equity - that's what gives it the potential for high returns. Then we add a 3-year lock-in period for flavor concentration. Finally, we glaze it with Section 80C tax benefits!"

Kumar: "Wow! So I can save taxes and potentially earn good returns?"

Chef: "Exactly! You can invest up to ₹1.5 lakhs per year in ELSS and deduct it from your taxable income under Section 80C. It's like getting a discount on a gourmet dessert!"

They put the ELSS Eclair in the oven.

Chef: "Remember, it needs to bake for at least 3 years. That's the lock-in period. But the longer you let it bake, the better it potentially tastes!"

Lesson: ELSS mutual funds offer tax deductions under Section 80C along with the potential for capital appreciation, but come with a mandatory 3-year lock-in period.

Scene 3: The Long-Term Capital Gains Lassi

They move to the beverage station.

Chef: "Now, let's make a refreshing Long-Term Capital Gains Lassi! This is for equity mutual funds held for more than one year."

Kumar starts blending ingredients.

Chef: "Pour in some equity mutual fund units, blend it for over a year, and voila! The first ₹1 lakh of your capital gains is completely tax-free. Anything above that is taxed at just 10%!"

Kumar takes a sip: "Mmm, tastes like financial freedom!"

Chef: "Indeed! And the best part? This concessional rate applies without indexation benefits. It's like getting a discount on an already refreshing drink!"

Lesson: Long-term capital gains from equity mutual funds enjoy favorable tax treatment, making them an attractive option for wealth creation.

Scene 4: The Debt Fund Dharana

They move to a zen corner of the kitchen with a slow cooker.

Chef: "Here's where we practice the art of patience with our Debt Fund Dharana. It's a slow-cooked dish that gets better with time."

Kumar adds ingredients to the slow cooker.

Chef: "For debt funds, the longer you cook, the better the tax flavor. Hold for over 3 years, and you get the benefit of indexation!"

Kumar: "Indexation? Is that like adding spices?"

Chef: "Sort of! It adjusts your purchase price for inflation, reducing your taxable gains. After 3 years, you pay only 20% tax on these inflation-adjusted gains. It's like magically reducing the calories in your dish!"

Lesson: Debt mutual funds held for over 3 years benefit from indexation, potentially leading to significant tax savings on long-term capital gains.

Scene 5: The Dividend Dehaat

They approach a rustic corner of the kitchen.

Chef: "Welcome to the Dividend Dehaat! Here, we'll see how dividends from mutual funds are served up tax-wise."

Kumar notices two plates: one labeled "Before 2020" and another "After 2020".

Chef: "Before 2020, dividends were like a tax-free prasad. But now, they're added to your income and taxed at your slab rate. It's like going from free village food to a billed thali!"

Kumar looks disappointed.

Chef: "Don't worry! This change encourages a growth-oriented approach. For regular income, consider systematic withdrawal plans instead of dividend options. It's like crafting your own balanced meal rather than depending on free samples!"

Lesson: With dividends now taxable, growth options in mutual funds may be more tax-efficient for many investors compared to dividend options.

Scene 6: The Tax Harvesting Tadka

They return to the main cooking station.

Chef: "Time for some Tax Harvesting Tadka! This is a technique to add flavor to your tax-saving dish."

Kumar watches as the chef demonstrates with two similar-looking funds.

Chef: "If you have capital gains in one equity fund, you can sell it and immediately buy a similar fund. This 'realizes' your gains up to the ₹1 lakh tax-free limit each year. It's like skimming the cream off your curry and adding it back for extra richness!"

Kumar: "That's clever! But isn't it like having the same dish?"

Chef: "Almost! But you're resetting your cost basis higher, potentially reducing future tax liability. Just ensure the funds are similar, not identical, to avoid 'wash sale' rules!"

Lesson: Tax harvesting can be an effective strategy to manage tax liability in equity mutual fund investments, but it should be done carefully and in compliance with tax laws.

Climax: The Tax-Efficient Investment Thali

They present a grand thali with all the dishes they've prepared.

Chef: "And here's our pièce de résistance - the Tax-Efficient Investment Thali! A balanced meal of ELSS for tax deductions, equity funds for long-term capital gains benefits, debt funds for indexation advantages, and clever serving techniques like tax harvesting."

Kumar looks at the thali in awe: "It's a feast for both the palate and the pocket!"

Chef: "Remember, Kumar, the key to a good financial diet is balance. Mix these tax-saving dishes wisely, and always consider your overall financial health, not just the tax flavor!"

Final Lesson: A well-planned mutual fund portfolio can offer significant tax advantages, but it should be tailored to your overall financial goals and risk appetite.

And cut! That's a wrap on "Tax Savings: The Sweet Chutney of Mutual Fund Investing"! Remember, dear viewers, in the grand buffet of investments, tax-saving mutual funds are the sweet chutney that can make your financial meal much more satisfying!

As the credits roll, we see Mutual Kumar confidently preparing his own tax-efficient investment thali, mixing ELSS eclairs with Long-Term Capital Gains Lassi and a side of Debt Fund Dharana.

10

Common Pitfalls: Avoiding the Potholes on Your Investment Highway

Navigating Investment Potholes: A Cautionary Drive

Lights, camera, action! Welcome to "The Great Indian Investment Road Trip," where we navigate the treacherous terrain of mutual fund investing! Join our hero, Mutual Kumar, as he embarks on a journey to avoid the potholes that have tripped up many investors before him.

Scene 1: The Investment Highway Departure

Mutual Kumar approaches a colorful Ambassador car with "Financial Freedom Express" painted on the side.

Road Trip Guide: "Welcome to The Great Indian Investment Road Trip, Kumar! Today, we'll cruise down the mutual fund highway, avoiding the potholes that have caused many a financial fender-bender. Ready to roll?"

Kumar: "Absolutely! But I'm a bit nervous about all these potential pitfalls."

Road Trip Guide: "Don't worry! We'll learn from others' mistakes. It's like having a GPS built on the experiences of lakhs of Indian investors!"

Lesson: Learning from common investment mistakes can help you navigate your financial journey more smoothly.

Scene 2: The Herd Mentality Hairpin Bend

They approach a sharp bend where a crowd of cars is following each other blindly.

Road Trip Guide: "Watch out! This is the Herd Mentality Hairpin Bend. Many investors crash here by blindly following the crowd."

They watch as a car with "Sharma ji ka Beta" written on it leads a group of vehicles into a ditch.

Kumar: "Oh no! What happened?"

Road Trip Guide: "That's the story of Rajesh from Mumbai. In 2017, he invested heavily in cryptocurrency funds just because everyone was doing it. When the crypto market crashed in 2018, so did his savings."

Kumar: "So, we shouldn't follow investment trends?"

Road Trip Guide: "Not blindly. Always understand what you're investing in and why it fits your goals."

Lesson: Avoid making investment decisions based solely on what others are doing. Your financial journey is unique to you.

Scene 3: The Short-Term Thinking Shortcut

They pass a tempting-looking shortcut that ends abruptly at a cliff.

Road Trip Guide: "Beware of the Short-Term Thinking Shortcut! Many investors try to get rich quick and end up falling off the cliff."

They see a car dangling off the edge with "Get Rich Quick" written on its side.

Road Trip Guide: "That's Priya from Bangalore. She kept switching between mutual funds every few months based on short-term performance. She ended up with high exit loads, taxes, and lower overall returns."

Kumar: "So, we should stick to our funds for the long term?"

Road Trip Guide: "Generally, yes. Mutual funds are marathons, not sprints. Give your investments time to grow."

Lesson: Avoid frequent switching based on short-term performance. Stay invested for the long term to reap the benefits of compounding and market cycles.

Scene 4: The Diversification Desert

They enter a barren stretch where all the cars look identical.

Road Trip Guide: "Welcome to the Diversification Desert. Investors who put all their money in one type of fund often get stranded here."

They spot a lone car with "Tech Fund Only" written on it, stuck in the sand.

Road Trip Guide: "That's Amit from Pune. During the IT boom, he invested all his savings in tech-focused funds. When the sector crashed in the early 2000s, his portfolio value was cut in half overnight."

Kumar: "So we should spread our investments across different types of funds?"

Road Trip Guide: "Exactly! Diversification is like having different types of vehicles for different terrains."

Lesson: Don't put all your eggs in one basket. Diversify across different types of mutual funds to balance risk and potential returns.

Scene 5: The Expense Ratio Expressway

They cruise down a smooth highway with toll booths of varying sizes.

Road Trip Guide: "This is the Expense Ratio Expressway. Many investors ignore these tolls, not realizing how they eat into returns over time."

They watch a car struggling to pass through a large toll booth labeled "High Expense Ratio."

Road Trip Guide: "That's Sunita from Delhi. She chose a fund with a 2.5% expense ratio because it had slightly higher past returns. Over 20 years, she lost nearly 20% of her potential wealth to these high fees."

Kumar: "Wow! So we should always go for the lowest expense ratio?"

Road Trip Guide: "Not always, but it's an important factor. Balance it with the fund's performance and your investment goals."

Lesson: Pay attention to expense ratios. Over long periods, even small differences in fees can significantly impact your returns.

Scene 6: The Panic Selling Pothole

They approach a massive pothole where cars are frantically reversing.

Road Trip Guide: "Watch out for the Panic Selling Pothole! This is where many investors lose their nerve during market downturns."

They see a car stuck in the pothole with "Sold at the Bottom" painted on its side.

Road Trip Guide: "That's Rahul from Kolkata. During the 2008 financial crisis, he sold all his equity funds in panic. He missed out on the market recovery and lost nearly 50% of his potential returns over the next decade."

Kumar: "So we should never sell during market crashes?"

Road Trip Guide: "It's not about never selling, but about not making decisions based on short-term fear. Stick to your long-term plan."

Lesson: Avoid making emotional decisions during market volatility. Stay focused on your long-term financial goals.

Scene 7: The Research Roundabout

They enter a roundabout filled with signboards showing fund information.

Road Trip Guide: "Welcome to the Research Roundabout. Many investors get dizzy here and make uninformed choices."

They spot a car going in circles, its driver looking confused at the plethora of information.

Road Trip Guide: "That's Anjali from Chennai. She invested in a fund just because it had a 5-star rating, without understanding its strategy or risk profile. The fund's performance didn't align with her conservative investment style, causing her sleepless nights during market volatility."

Kumar: "So ratings aren't everything?"

Road Trip Guide: "They're a starting point, not the end. Always understand what you're investing in and why it fits your goals."

Lesson: Don't rely solely on ratings or past performance. Do thorough research and understand a fund's strategy and risk profile before investing.

Climax: The Balanced Portfolio Bridge

They finally reach a sturdy bridge that leads to "Financial Freedom City."

Road Trip Guide: "Congratulations, Kumar! We've reached the Balanced Portfolio Bridge. This is where smart investors create a well-rounded investment strategy that can weather any market condition."

They observe various cars crossing the bridge smoothly, each representing a balanced mix of different mutual fund types.

Kumar: "I see! So a well-planned portfolio helps avoid these pitfalls?"

Road Trip Guide: "Exactly! It's about creating an investment strategy that aligns with your goals, risk tolerance, and time horizon. And remember, regular review and rebalancing are key to staying on track."

Final Lesson: Building a balanced, diversified portfolio aligned with your financial goals, regularly reviewing and rebalancing it, and staying disciplined during market fluctuations are key to successful mutual fund investing.

And cut! That's a wrap on "Common Pitfalls: Avoiding the Potholes on Your Investment Highway"! Remember, dear viewers, in the great road trip of mutual fund investing, it's not about avoiding every bump in the road, but about having a sturdy vehicle (balanced portfolio) and a reliable map (informed strategy) to reach your financial destination safely!

As the credits roll, we see Mutual Kumar confidently charting his investment route, equipped with the knowledge to navigate around common pitfalls and cruise towards his financial goals.

11

Your Mutual Fund Toolkit: Essentials for Every Indian Investor

Empowering Your Investment Journey: The Indian Toolkit

Lights, camera, action! Welcome to "Mission: Mutual Fund,"

where our hero Mutual Kumar transforms into Agent MF007, assembling a cutting-edge toolkit for his mutual fund investment mission. Join us as he gathers the essential gadgets and intel sources for every Indian mutual fund investor!

Scene 1: The Secret Briefing

Agent MF007 (our Mutual Kumar) enters a dimly lit room where M (Mutual Fund Mastermind) awaits.

M: "Welcome, Agent MF007. Your mission, should you choose to accept it, is to build the ultimate mutual fund toolkit for Indian investors. Are you ready?"

MF007: "Ready and willing, M. What's my first gadget?"

M: "Let's start with your research arsenal. Follow me to the lab."

Lesson: Building a comprehensive toolkit is crucial for successful mutual fund investing.

Scene 2: The Research Radar

They enter a high-tech lab filled with screens and blinking gadgets.

M: "First up, your Research Radar. These are essential websites for fund analysis and comparison."

1. Value Research Online Viewer M demonstrates a sleek tablet: "This device gives you access to ValueResearchOnline.com. It's like X-ray vision for mutual funds - you can see right through their performance, ratings, and portfolio holdings."
2. Morning Star Magnifier M hands over a sophisticated

monocle: "The MorningStar.in lens. It provides in-depth fund analysis, helping you spot the stars in the mutual fund universe."

3. CRISIL Ranking Recorder A smartwatch-like device beeps. M explains: "The CRISIL Mutual Fund Ranking watch. It gives you quarterly rankings of funds, helping you track the top performers."

MF007 tries on the gadgets: "Impressive! But how do I make sense of all this data?"

M: "That's where your next tool comes in - the Financial Ratio Analyzer."

Lesson: Websites like Value Research, Morningstar, and CRISIL provide valuable data and analysis for mutual fund research.

Scene 3: The Financial Ratio Analyzer

M unveils a complex-looking calculator.

M: "This is your Financial Ratio Analyzer. It helps you crunch the numbers that matter."

MF007 examines the device, noticing buttons labeled 'Expense Ratio', 'Sharpe Ratio', 'Alpha', and 'Beta'.

M: "The Expense Ratio button helps you compare fund costs. Sharpe Ratio measures risk-adjusted returns. Alpha shows a fund's excess return compared to its benchmark, while Beta measures its volatility."

MF007: "So this helps me go beyond just returns and dig deeper into fund performance?"

M: "Exactly! In the mutual fund world, these ratios are your secret code to fund quality."

Lesson: Understanding key financial ratios is crucial for evaluating mutual fund performance and risk.

Scene 4: The AMC Archives

They approach a massive vault door.

M: "This is the AMC Archive. It holds the secret files of every Asset Management Company in India."

The vault opens to reveal a library of fund house websites and factsheets.

M: "Always go straight to the source. AMC websites provide the most up-to-date fund information, scheme information documents, and factsheets."

MF007 browses through some factsheets: "This is great for due diligence!"

M: "Indeed. Now, let's move on to your communication devices."

Lesson: AMC websites and factsheets are primary sources for accurate and detailed fund information.

Scene 5: The Market News Multiverse

They enter a room with screens showing various news channels and websites.

M: "Welcome to the Market News Multiverse. Staying informed is crucial for your mission."

1. Economic Times Market Scanner A newspaper that updates in real-time: "This scans the latest market news and mutual fund updates."
2. Moneycontrol Monitoring Device A smartwatch that flashes breaking news: "For real-time market movements

and expert opinions."

3. CNBC-TV18 Communicator A small earpiece: "For audio updates and expert interviews on the go."

MF007: "With these, I'll always be in the know!"

M: "Exactly. But remember, use these for information, not for panic-driven decisions."

Lesson: *Staying updated with financial news helps in making informed investment decisions, but avoid reacting to every market movement.*

Scene 6: The Trading Terminal

They approach a high-tech computer setup.

M: "Now for the most crucial part of your toolkit - the Trading Terminal. This is where you'll execute your mutual fund transactions."

MF007: "Multiple screens? Looks complicated."

M: "Not at all. Each screen represents a different mutual fund platform. Let's take a tour."

1. Groww Gizmo A user-friendly tablet: "The Groww app - simple, intuitive, great for beginners."
2. Kuvera Kaleidoscope A sleek laptop: "Kuvera platform - offers direct plans and smart insights."
3. Zerodha Coin Zapper A streamlined smartphone: "Zerodha Coin - seamless integration with trading accounts."
4. PayTM Money Mobilizer Another smartphone: "PayTM Money - convenient for those already in the PayTM ecosystem."
5. ET Money Encoder A versatile smartwatch: "ET Money -

good for goal-based investing and tracking."

MF007 tries each device: "These make investing seem so accessible!"

M: "Indeed. Choose the one that feels most comfortable for you. Remember, the best platform is the one you'll actually use consistently."

Lesson: There are various user-friendly platforms available for mutual fund investing in India. Choose one that aligns with your needs and comfort level.

Scene 7: The Regulatory Roundtable

They enter a room with a round table, each seat representing a regulatory body.

M: "Your final stop - the Regulatory Roundtable. Always keep these authorities on your radar."

1. SEBI Surveillance System A powerful telescope: "For viewing SEBI's website. Keep an eye on regulations and investor education materials."
2. AMFI Analyzer A codex that updates automatically: "Access to AMFI's website for industry standards and best practices."

MF007: "So these help me stay compliant and informed about industry standards?"

M: "Precisely. In the world of investing, knowledge of regulations is your best protection."

Lesson: Staying informed about regulations and industry standards is crucial for responsible investing.

Climax: The Mission Briefcase

M hands MF007 a sleek briefcase.

M: "And finally, your Mission Briefcase. It contains all the tools we've discussed, ready for your mutual fund adventure."

MF007 opens it, seeing compartments for each tool: "This is incredible! I feel ready to take on the mutual fund world."

M: "Remember, Agent MF007, these tools are powerful, but your most important asset is your judgment. Use these wisely, stay disciplined, and your mission to financial freedom will be a success."

Final Lesson: While tools and platforms are essential, successful mutual fund investing ultimately depends on the investor's judgment, discipline, and consistent use of available resources.

And cut! That's a wrap on "Your Mutual Fund Toolkit: Essentials for Every Indian Investor"! Remember, dear viewers, in the thrilling world of mutual fund investing, you too can be Agent MF007 - equipped with the right tools, intelligence, and platforms to accomplish your financial mission!

As the credits roll, we see Agent MF007 (our Mutual Kumar) confidently using his new toolkit, researching funds, analyzing ratios, and making informed investment decisions on his chosen platform.

12

Building Your Financial Thali: Balancing Mutual Funds in Your Portfolio

Financial Feast: Crafting Your Investment Thali

Lights, camera, action! Welcome to "The Great Indian Financial

Feast," where creating a diversified investment portfolio is as exciting as preparing for a grand Indian wedding banquet! Join our hero, Mutual Kumar, as he learns the art of building the perfect financial thali with the help of Master Chef Vijaya, the seasoned portfolio manager!

Scene 1: The Financial Kitchen

Mutual Kumar enters a bustling kitchen filled with various ingredients and cooking stations.

Master Chef Vijaya: "Welcome to our Financial Kitchen, Kumar! Today, we'll prepare the most important meal of your life - your investment portfolio thali. Are you ready to cook up a storm?"

Kumar: "Absolutely, Chef! But I'm a bit overwhelmed by all these ingredients."

Chef Vijaya: "Don't worry! We'll go through each component step by step. Remember, a balanced thali is key to a satisfying financial meal!"

Lesson: Creating a diversified investment portfolio is like preparing a balanced meal, with each component playing a crucial role.

Scene 2: The Equity Entree

They approach a sizzling grill labeled "Equity Station."

Chef Vijaya: "Let's start with our main course - the Equity Entree. It's the growth engine of your financial thali."

Kumar: "Smells exciting, but also a bit spicy!"

Chef Vijaya: "Indeed! Equity mutual funds can add spice to your returns, but they can also be volatile. Let's prepare a mix."

They start cooking:

1. Large-cap Lamb Curry: "Stable and reliable, like blue-chip companies."
2. Mid-cap Masala Dosa: "Potential for higher growth, but with added risk."
3. Small-cap Spicy Kebabs: "Exciting growth prospects, but handle with care!"

Chef Vijaya: "The key is to balance these based on your risk appetite and investment horizon. For a young investor like you, we might make equity about 60-70% of your thali."

Lesson: Equity mutual funds form the core of long-term wealth creation in a portfolio, but the allocation should be based on individual risk tolerance and investment goals.

Scene 3: The Debt Daal

They move to a slow-cooking station labeled "Debt Corner."

Chef Vijaya: "Now for our Debt Daal - the stability factor in your financial diet."

Kumar: "Looks less exciting than the equity dishes."

Chef Vijaya: "Ah, but it's essential! Debt funds are like comfort food - they provide stability and regular income to your portfolio."

They prepare:

1. Government Securities Ghee Daal: "Ultra-safe, but with modest returns."
2. Corporate Bond Tadka Daal: "Slightly higher returns, with a bit more risk."
3. Short-term Debt Daal Fry: "For your short-term financial needs."

Chef Vijaya: "For someone your age, we might allocate about 20-30% to debt funds. As you grow older, you'll likely increase this portion for more stability."

Lesson: Debt mutual funds provide stability and regular income in a portfolio, acting as a counterbalance to the volatility of equity investments.

Scene 4: The Hybrid Halwa

They approach a mixing station where different ingredients are being combined.

Chef Vijaya: "Here's where we make our Hybrid Halwa - a perfect blend of equity and debt."

Kumar watches as Chef Vijaya mixes ingredients from both the Equity and Debt stations.

Chef Vijaya: "Balanced funds or hybrid funds are like this halwa - they offer a pre-mixed combination of equity and debt. They're great for investors who want a readymade balanced dish."

Kumar tastes it: "Mmm, not too spicy, not too bland. Just right!"

Chef Vijaya: "Exactly! These can form about 10-15% of your thali, especially if you're unsure about balancing equity and debt yourself."

Lesson: Hybrid mutual funds offer a pre-balanced mix of equity and debt, suitable for investors seeking a readymade diversified option.

Scene 5: The International Chutney

They move to a exotic-looking corner of the kitchen.

Chef Vijaya: "Time to add some international flavor with our Global Chutney!"

Kumar: "Global flavors in my Indian thali?"

Chef Vijaya: "Absolutely! International or global funds invest in markets outside India, adding a different taste to your portfolio."

They prepare a small bowl of colorful chutney.

Chef Vijaya: "We'll add just a dollop - say 5-10% of your thali. It helps in geographical diversification and can balance out risks specific to the Indian market."

Lesson: International mutual funds add geographical diversification to a portfolio, potentially reducing country-specific risks.

Scene 6: The Liquid Fund Raita

They reach a cooling station with various beverages.

Chef Vijaya: "Every good thali needs a cooling Raita. In our financial thali, that's the Liquid Fund Raita."

Kumar: "For emergencies, right?"

Chef Vijaya: "Exactly! Liquid funds are like financial raita - cool, readily available, and perfect for short-term needs or emergencies."

They prepare a bowl of raita.

Chef Vijaya: "We'll keep about 5-10% of your thali as liquid funds. It's your financial emergency stash."

Lesson: Liquid funds serve as an emergency fund and for short-term financial needs in a diversified portfolio.

Scene 7: The Gold Fund Dessert

They approach a glittering dessert counter.

Chef Vijaya: "And for a touch of traditional security, let's add a Gold Fund Dessert."

Kumar: "Gold in a mutual fund?"

Chef Vijaya: "Yes! Gold mutual funds or ETFs give you exposure to gold without the hassle of physical storage. It's like having the sweetness of gold in an easy-to-consume form."

They add a small, shimmering dessert to the thali.

Chef Vijaya: "A small portion - about 5% of your thali - can act as a hedge against inflation and economic uncertainties."

Lesson: Gold mutual funds can serve as a hedge against inflation and economic uncertainties in a diversified portfolio.

Climax: Assembling Your Financial Thali

They bring all the prepared dishes to a large serving area.

Chef Vijaya: "Now, Kumar, it's time to assemble your Financial Thali!"

Kumar starts arranging the dishes, guided by Chef Vijaya.

Chef Vijaya: "Remember, the exact proportions depend on your taste (risk appetite), dietary restrictions (financial goals), and digestive capacity (investment horizon). This thali should be reviewed and adjusted periodically as your life situations change."

Kumar looks at his completed thali with pride: "It looks delicious and well-balanced!"

Chef Vijaya: "Indeed! And just like a good meal plan, your financial plan should include regular review and rebalancing. As you grow older or your goals change, you might want to adjust the spiciness (risk) of your thali."

Final Lesson: A well-diversified investment portfolio, like a balanced thali, should be tailored to individual needs, regularly reviewed, and adjusted as personal circumstances change.

And cut! That's a wrap on "Building Your Financial Thali: Balancing Mutual Funds in Your Portfolio"! Remember, dear viewers, in the grand feast of financial planning, your investment portfolio should be as diverse and well-balanced as a perfect Indian thali!

As the credits roll, we see Mutual Kumar confidently explaining his new financial thali to his family, pointing out how each mutual fund plays a crucial role in his overall financial diet.

13

The Road Ahead: Future of Mutual Funds in India

Pathway to Prosperity: India's Mutual Fund Future

Lights, camera, action! Welcome to "Mutual Fund 2050: A

Financial Odyssey," where we take a thrilling journey into the future of India's mutual fund industry! Join our hero, Mutual Kumar, as he time-travels to explore emerging trends and navigate the impact of economic and regulatory changes!

Scene 1: The Time Machine Launch

Mutual Kumar approaches a glittering time machine shaped like a giant mutual fund portfolio.

Dr. Future Fund: "Welcome, Kumar! Ready to explore the future of mutual funds in India?"

Kumar: "Absolutely, Doctor! But will my current mutual fund knowledge be outdated?"

Dr. Future Fund: "Some things change, some remain the same. Let's find out!"

They step into the time machine, which whirs to life with flashy lights and Bollywood-style background music.

Lesson: The mutual fund industry is dynamic, with both evolving trends and enduring principles.

Scene 2: The Digital Revolution Plaza

They emerge in a futuristic city square where everyone is managing investments through holographic interfaces.

Dr. Future Fund: "Welcome to the Digital Revolution Plaza! Notice how technology has transformed investing?"

Kumar watches in awe as people make investments with voice commands and gesture controls.

AI Assistant (popping up): "Based on your brainwave patterns, I recommend increasing your SIP in the Quantum Computing Fund by 5%."

Kumar: "Wow! So personal finance has become hyper-personalized?"

Dr. Future Fund: "Indeed! AI and machine learning have made portfolio management incredibly sophisticated and tailored to individual needs."

Lesson: The future of mutual funds will likely see increased use of AI and machine learning for personalized investment advice and portfolio management.

Scene 3: The Sustainable Investing Skyway

They float up to a green, tree-lined skyway where fund managers are excitedly discussing sustainability metrics.

Dr. Future Fund: "This is the Sustainable Investing Skyway. ESG funds have become mainstream!"

Kumar overhears conversations: Fund Manager 1: "Our Carbon Neutral Tech Fund has outperformed the market by 20%!" Fund Manager 2: "The new Circular Economy Index is revolutionizing how we measure sustainability."

Kumar: "So green is the new black in investing?"

Dr. Future Fund: "Exactly! Environmental, Social, and Governance (ESG) factors are now central to investment decisions. Regulatory changes have made sustainability reporting mandatory for all companies."

Lesson: Sustainable and ESG investing is likely to become increasingly important in the future of mutual funds.

Scene 4: The Crypto-Commodities Exchange

They enter a bustling exchange where traditional and digital assets are being traded side by side.

Dr. Future Fund: "Welcome to the Crypto-Commodities Exchange! The definition of 'asset class' has expanded."

Kumar sees funds trading in cryptocurrencies, digital real estate, and even "data commodities."

Trader: "The Bitcoin-Backed Mutual Fund is up 10%, while the Data Mining Index has surged 15%!"

Kumar: "Are these still considered alternative investments?"

Dr. Future Fund: "Not anymore! Regulatory clarity has brought these assets into the mainstream. Mutual funds now routinely include crypto and digital assets for diversification."

Lesson: The future may see mutual funds incorporating a wider range of assets, including cryptocurrencies and other digital assets, subject to regulatory approvals.

Scene 5: The Global Investment Gateway

They step onto a platform where investors are seamlessly putting money into funds across the globe.

Dr. Future Fund: "This is the Global Investment Gateway. Geographical boundaries in investing have blurred significantly."

Kumar watches an investor casually putting money into a "Pan-Asian Smart Cities Fund" and a "Latin American Renewable Energy Fund."

Kumar: "International investing seems so easy now!"

Dr. Future Fund: "Indeed! Regulatory changes have simplified cross-border investments. Indian investors now have much easier access to global opportunities, and vice versa."

Lesson: The future of mutual funds in India may involve greater integration with global markets and easier access to international investment opportunities.

Scene 6: The Micro-Investing Mela

They visit a lively fair where people from all walks of life are engaging in investing activities.

Dr. Future Fund: "Welcome to the Micro-Investing Mela! Mutual funds have become truly accessible to all."

Kumar sees street vendors, students, and daily wage workers all using simple apps to invest small amounts.

App Announcement: "Congratulations! Your ₹10 investment in the Fractional Real Estate Fund is confirmed!"

Kumar: "Mutual funds for everyone, literally!"

Dr. Future Fund: "Absolutely! Regulatory changes and technology have enabled micro-investing. Now, anyone can start investing with as little as ₹1."

Lesson: The future may see even greater democratization of mutual fund investing, with micro-investing becoming commonplace.

Scene 7: The Regulatory Roundtable

They enter a holographic conference room where regulators, fund managers, and AI systems are in deep discussion.

Dr. Future Fund: "This is the Regulatory Roundtable. The approach to regulation has evolved significantly."

Kumar listens in: Regulator: "Our AI systems have detected a potential risk in the Quantum Computing Fund. Let's proactively adjust the risk parameters." AI System: "Agreed. I've already drafted the necessary disclosure documents for investor approval."

Kumar: "Real-time regulation?"

Dr. Future Fund: "Yes! Regulation has become more dynamic and proactive, leveraging technology to protect investor interests while fostering innovation."

Lesson: The regulatory landscape for mutual funds is likely to evolve, potentially becoming more dynamic and technology-driven.

Climax: The Future Finance Festival

They arrive at a grand celebration of financial literacy and inclusion.

Dr. Future Fund: "Welcome to the Future Finance Festival! This is where we celebrate how far we've come in financial awareness and inclusion."

Kumar sees people from all backgrounds confidently discussing investment strategies, robots offering personalized financial education, and holographic displays showing the positive impact of widespread mutual fund adoption on India's economy.

Kumar: "This is incredible! Mutual funds seem to have transformed India's financial landscape!"

Dr. Future Fund: "Indeed! But remember, while the tools and technologies have changed, the core principles remain: disciplined investing, diversification, and aligning investments with personal goals."

Final Lesson: While the future of mutual funds in India looks exciting with technological advancements and new investment avenues, the fundamental principles of wise investing are likely to remain relevant.

And cut! That's a wrap on "The Road Ahead: Future of

Mutual Funds in India"! Remember, dear viewers, while we can't predict the future with certainty, we can prepare for it by staying informed, adaptable, and grounded in sound financial principles!

As the credits roll, we see Mutual Kumar back in the present, excitedly sharing his vision of the future with his friends and family, encouraging them to start their mutual fund journey today to be ready for the exciting possibilities of tomorrow.